CAMBRIDGE LIBRARY COLLECTION

Books of enduring scholarly value

Religion

For centuries, scripture and theology were the focus of prodigious amounts of scholarship and publishing, dominated in the English-speaking world by the work of Protestant Christians. Enlightenment philosophy and science, anthropology, ethnology and the colonial experience all brought new perspectives, lively debates and heated controversies to the study of religion and its role in the world, many of which continue to this day. This series explores the editing and interpretation of religious texts, the history of religious ideas and institutions, and not least the encounter between religion and science.

The Relations of Science and Religion

First published in both New York and London in 1881, at a time of heated debates over the relationship between science and religion, this book arose from Henry Calderwood's Morse lectures given in association with Union Theological Seminary, New York in 1880. Calderwood, a Scottish clergyman, was professor of moral philosophy at Edinburgh University for over thirty years. He published on a wide range of subjects, and devoted several books to the science/religion question, taking the line that theism and evolution were compatible. The present volume provides evidence of the lively international dimension of the late nineteenth-century intellectual engagement with evolutionary theory and related scientific and philosophical developments, and is a valuable resource for historians of the subject and those revisiting the arguments today.

Cambridge University Press has long been a pioneer in the reissuing of out-of-print titles from its own backlist, producing digital reprints of books that are still sought after by scholars and students but could not be reprinted economically using traditional technology. The Cambridge Library Collection extends this activity to a wider range of books which are still of importance to researchers and professionals, either for the source material they contain, or as landmarks in the history of their academic discipline.

Drawing from the world-renowned collections in the Cambridge University Library, and guided by the advice of experts in each subject area, Cambridge University Press is using state-of-the-art scanning machines in its own Printing House to capture the content of each book selected for inclusion. The files are processed to give a consistently clear, crisp image, and the books finished to the high quality standard for which the Press is recognised around the world. The latest print-on-demand technology ensures that the books will remain available indefinitely, and that orders for single or multiple copies can quickly be supplied.

The Cambridge Library Collection will bring back to life books of enduring scholarly value (including out-of-copyright works originally issued by other publishers) across a wide range of disciplines in the humanities and social sciences and in science and technology.

The Relations of Science and Religion

The Morse Lecture, 1880

Henry Calderwood

CAMBRIDGE UNIVERSITY PRESS

Cambridge, New York, Melbourne, Madrid, Cape Town, Singapore,
São Paolo, Delhi, Dubai, Tokyo

Published in the United States of America by Cambridge University Press, New York

www.cambridge.org
Information on this title: www.cambridge.org/9781108000154

This edition first published 1881
This digitally printed version 2009

ISBN 978-1-108-00015-4 Paperback

RELATIONS OF SCIENCE AND RELIGION.

THE RELATIONS

OF

SCIENCE AND RELIGION.

The Morse Lecture, 1880,

CONNECTED WITH THE UNION THEOLOGICAL SEMINARY, NEW YORK.

BY

HENRY CALDERWOOD, LL.D.,

PROFESSOR OF MORAL PHILOSOPHY, UNIVERSITY OF EDINBURGH, AUTHOR OF "RELATIONS OF MIND AND BRAIN," ETC.

London

MACMILLAN AND CO.

1881

EXTRACT FROM THE DEED OF TRUST, ESTABLISHING THE MORSE LECTURESHIP.

"The general subject of the Lectures, I desire to be:

"The relation of the Bible to any of the Sciences, as Geography, Geology, History, and Ethnology, the vindication of the inspiration and authenticity of the Bible, against attacks made on scientific grounds, and the relation of the facts and truths contained in the Word of God, to the principles, methods and aims of any of the Sciences.

"Upon one or more of these topics a course of ten public Lectures shall be given at least once in two or three years, by a Lecturer, ordinarily to be chosen two years in advance of the time for delivering of the Lectures.

"The appointment of the Lecturer shall be by the concurrent action of the Founder of the Lectureship, during his life, the Board of Directors, and the faculty of said Seminary.

"The funds shall be securely invested, and the interest of the same shall be devoted to the payment of the Lecturer, and to the publication of the Lectures within a year after the delivery of the same.

"The copyright of the Lectures shall be vested in the Seminary."

(Signed) SAMUEL F. B. MORSE.

PREFACE.

The aim of the present volume is to indicate the measure of harmony traceable between recent advances in science, and the fundamental character istics of religious thought, and the extent to which harmony is possible. This attempt has been made in the hope of contributing towards a better understanding of the relative positions of scientists and theologians, thereby aiding the formation of public opinion on questions appearing to involve serious antagonism.

The plan followed is to bring under review the great fields of scientific inquiry, advancing from unorganized existence to Man; to present the most recent results of research in these separate fields, without extending to minute details; as far as possible, to allow scientific observers to state results in their own words; and then to examine carefully the reasonings deduced from ascertained facts, and the bearing of facts and inferences on religious thought.

The general result is that marked modifications of thought concerning the structure and order of the universe have arisen on account of scientific discoveries, to be accepted by theologians, as by all thinkers; that the bearing of these modifications on religious conceptions has been greatly mistaken by many scientific observers; and that it must be held clear by scientists and theologians alike, that while scientific methods are reliable within their own spheres, science can bear no testimony, and can offer no criticism, as to the supernatural, inasmuch as science is only an explanation of ascertained facts by recognition of natural law. In accordance with this last statement, it is maintained, that science does not reach, far less deal with, the problem concerning the origin of Nature, the solution of which can be found only by transcending Nature, that is, by recognizing the supernatural.

In the course followed I believe the purpose of the eminent Physicist who founded the lecture, has been rigidly kept in view.

I desire here to express to the President and Professors of Union Theological Seminary, my sense of their great kindness while I delivered the course of lectures in New York, and specially for so arranging as to allow of including the full course within eight lectures,—a form which has been retained in publication.

I have also to express my thanks for the kind manner in which these lectures were received in Edinburgh, where, with the exception of the two first, the course was, by request, redelivered.

H. C.

UNIVERSITY OF EDINBURGH,
January 31st, 1881.

CONTENTS.

LECTURE I.

Conditions of the Inquiry.

LECTURE II.

Experience gathered from Past Conflicts.

LECTURE III.

INORGANIC ELEMENTS IN THE UNIVERSE.

LECTURE IV.

ORGANIZED EXISTENCE. LIFE AND ITS DEVELOPMENT.

LECTURE V.

RELATIONS OF LOWER AND HIGHER ORGANISMS.

LECTURE VI.

HIGHER ORGANISMS;—RESEMBLANCES AND CONTRASTS.

LECTURE VII.

MAN'S PLACE IN THE WORLD.

LECTURE VIII.

DIVINE INTERPOSITION FOR MORAL GOVERNMENT.

APPENDIX.

RELATIONS OF SCIENCE AND RELIGION.

LECTURE I.

CONDITIONS OF THE INQUIRY.

AMONG the many advantages enjoyed by the present generation, one of the most conspicuous is that arising from the large advance made in physical science. The high value of this is apparent from whatever standpoint it is regarded. The vastly wider range of knowledge, the increase of appliances for inquiry, the greater facilities for work of all kinds, the freer intercommunion of all the divisions of our race, and the greater altitude from which the whole realm of existence can be contemplated; all these involve an immense gain for the present century.

With these advantages, however, there comes the difficulty of using them aright, a difficulty which we may expect to be greater when we are dealing with wider and more general aspects of existence, than when we are concerned with more restricted ranges of knowledge. It may be a much easier thing to state precisely how recent advances have affected a particular branch of science, such as astronomy or geology, than to say how they bear upon the general conception of the universe. Yet, while the latter is the more difficult question, it is that with which men generally must be more concerned. Only a very limited number of men can belong to the ranks of specialists devoted to a single branch of science. All men, specialists as well as others, are concerned with the wider question as to the true conception of the universe, and the bearing it has on human life and destiny. It is impossible to imagine that marked advance can be made in any of the sciences, without its having some bearing on the more general problem in which all men are practically interested. Each specialist perceives this more or less clearly as he is working out the result of complicated observations or calculations. The public mind may be said rather to *feel* that some modification of common belief is taking place, while there is great uncertainty as to the actual change. What gives a sense of security to the general conviction of educated men is that all increase of knowledge is clear gain, and that all advance is secured on familiar and well-tried lines. Progress is transition, and in a sense unsettling; but it is also accumulation, and thus in a more enduring sense, consolidating. Fresh observation in some one department of research does not overthrow all that was credited previously. It extends the area of knowledge, or carries us into a more minute acquaintance with particulars, and only in a restricted way modifies accepted positions, by introducing relations formerly unrecognized. Thus, progress in a particular science does not unsettle scientific belief.

In a manner exactly analogous, because resting on the same intellectual conditions, the combined advance of the whole order of sciences does not unsettle the mass of conviction belonging to instructed and ordinarily reflective men. It must, indeed, modify the form of general conviction, as it quickens intellectual interest, for the public mind receives, not reluctantly but gladly, additional results gathered under carefully tested scientific methods. This is nothing more than saying, that love of truth, and submission to the laws of evidence, are characteristic of all disciplined intelligence. Scientific inquirers are the trained instructors of the race, and others receive what they communicate, with true sense of its abiding worth. At the same time, such inquirers work from an intellectual basis which is common to all, finding application in all fields of activity. Upon that basis all men lean as they shape and regulate their life, finding themselves involved in disaster, or confirmed in a wise course, according as they are partial or thorough in their adherence to the conditions of rational life. As the mass of human interests can not be isolated from the results discovered in the path of advancing science; so neither can any form of inquiry be separated from the conditions which are common to all intellectual life, including even the least cultivated. So it happens that the race as a whole has a clear share in all the products of science, such as it has not in the products of industry. Rational conditions provide for a community of interest in intellectual work and results, greater than can be approached by all the value of material production.

These few general and very obvious considerations bring us into direct line with the relations of religion and science. Religion has a rational basis, as the condition of its practical worth. It takes its start from that common intellectual basis, which affords to science its essential conditions. Religion and science are exactly alike in these respects, that both present a body of harmonized conceptions, a clearly defined circle of intelligible statements, and both have a definite bearing on human action. Their practical value depends upon conformity with the common requirements of intelligence, and harmony with recognized fact. I place this declaration in the foreground of the present discussion, not only as a clear avowal of the footing on which religion presents its claims to acceptance, but more especially as a distinct and broad acknowledgment that the whole range of tests afforded by the entire circle of the sciences is legitimately applied to religion, and is to be deliberately met.

The object of the present course of lectures is to consider the relations of science to the Christian religion, as authoritatively revealed in the Bible, and as understood and accepted by those who profess themselves Christians, in grateful acknowledgment of what the Scriptures declare. The relations now to be dealt with are those subsisting between religion as presented in the Bible, (which is in the hands of all, to be examined and dealt with by scientific inquirers), and science as presented to us in the present day, for the acceptance of all. The claim to universal acceptance found here on both sides, is that which gives special interest and true logical importance to the problem. Christianity professes to discover a religion to be accepted of all men, and a practice to be observed by all: science professes to give an account of the state of things around us in the world, to be accepted by all, and acknowledged in practice if men would adapt themselves to the natural conditions of their life. This claim to universal acceptance is not affected on either side by the fact that diversities of interpretation and application emerge among the upholders of Christianity, and the expounders of science. Such diversities are well known to exist in both spheres of thought. It needs to be recognized at all times, and prominently stated in such a discussion as the present, that under the conditions determining the attainment of knowledge, there must be diversity of opinion. Indeed, the wider the area of acquired truth, the more extensive becomes the field of possible differences, both in respect of what is involved under conclusions already reached, and of what may transcend the boundaries of present knowledge. It is, therefore, no marvel that there is large diversity of opinion among scientific men, on many problems arising out of universally accepted positions. It is only by the same necessity that there is diversity of opinion on matters of religion. The materials of study are set before us in the mass, and our knowledge is to be obtained by the slow processes of intellectual procedure, in accordance with which some things become clear, while many more remain obscure. Whether we are dealing with book knowledge, or with knowledge obtained by direct observation of existing things, does not affect this matter. The intellectual conditions are the same in both cases, and it is from exactly the same intellectual source that inevitable conflict of opinion arises.

The simple and obvious truth is that there can be no field of human inquiry in which diversity of opinion can be avoided, for two reasons, that all knowledge possessed by us is incomplete, and active intelligence can not rest in the incomplete. Neither science nor theology can afford to dispense with hypothesis, that is conjecture, and where conjecture is, there is a wide region for devious wandering. Conjecture means inquiry into the unknown, and this is essential to intellectual life, equally necessary for science and religion, and accordingly diversity of opinion is inevitable in the history of both, as in the history of all forms of human activity. In every region of human knowledge there is a realm of the certain, and another of the uncertain, and accordingly there is diversity of opinion and conviction. Occasionally, in controversial writing, it is suggested that there is greater diversity of view in matters religious, than in matters scientific; and it is implied that such diversity is a reasonable ground of reproach. Both allegations are at fault, and the error arises from want of observation, involving imperfect acquaintance with the facts. Religion as it is concerned with the life of man himself, and is the subject of interest to all, has not only its common positions generally recognized, but also many of its phases of conflicting thought.

Science, as it is beyond the range of the great majority as a subject of personal research, and within reach of only a limited number as a subject even of book knowledge, has its questions of conflict concealed to some extent from the public view. But, even moderate acquaintance with science makes us aware of the fact that there is conflict of opinion in every region of inquiry. Indeed it should be alien to the reflective observer, to marvel at the discovery of diversity of thought in any region, or to make its existence a ground for adverse criticism. Commonly accepted conclusions must afford the basis for competent criticism, whatever be the field of inquiry brought under review; diversity of opinion beyond and around these, must be accepted as the uniform attendant of human knowledge, indicating at once the provision for intellectual progress and the inducement to it. Thus, on grounds indisputable from a scientific basis, we escape the need for vindicating religion from the charge of having its claims to rational homage weakened, by the diversity of opinion found within the boundaries of religious thought. Such diversity is in strict accordance with familiar facts connected with every branch of science. Whatever may be said of the strong and paradoxical, because one-sided, utterance of Lessing,* it must be manifest that in all directions we are of necessity searchers after truth, and it is in such circumstances an intellectual weakness to object to the reliability of generally accepted conclusions, because they become starting-points for many lines of conflicting speculation. In religious thought, as in scientific, there are on all hands the marks of the unfinished; and the varieties of opinion associated with generally accepted conviction only afford needful evidence of healthy intellectual activity.

As we daily hear much of the conflict between science and religion, and as it is one part of the purpose of the present course to deal with what is loudly proclaimed to be a serious feature in modern thought, it becomes needful to clear the ground considerably, with the view of discovering where the alleged con-

* "If God had held all truth in his right hand, and in his left the ever-living desire for truth, although with the condition that I should remain in error for ever, and if he should say to me 'choose,' I should humbly incline towards his left, and say, 'Father, give: pure truth is for thee alone?'"—*Wolfenbüttel Fragments.* See Zimmern's *Life of Lessing*, p. 361.

flict is, and what form it assumes. In this, as in many conflicts, there is much more din and tumult, than damage. We shall by and by hear much less of *conflict* than we are hearing at present. Meanwhile, however, the work is considerable which needs to be done in clearing the field, tracing boundaries, and disclosing the exact position of parties. In the ruder warfare of nations, this clearing work is undertaken by the combatants themselves, and if not accomplished by preliminary measures, it is at length achieved by the actual events of the struggle. But in this case, it may be done quietly enough by non-combatants, while it may contribute largely to the restricting of the conflict, and the establishment of peace. This I desire to attempt, in the hope that some service may be rendered both to the scientific, and non-scientific, by contributing towards a general understanding of the actual position of affairs. A quiet survey of events occurring during the last twenty-five years or so, which have influenced the relations of science and religion, may suffice to convince us that there has been on both sides needless planting of batteries, and pouring forth of shot. In many cases, the shot has only sunk into sand banks with no other result than heavy expenditure; in other cases, it has only shattered timber defences which were going at any rate, and soon to be abandoned. The worst result has been that the whole district around has been thrown into trouble under fear of disastrous results. This description must be held to apply to outbreaks of theological fury, as well as of scientific. I apprehend that there are few friends of religion conversant with the higher phases of intellectual life during the period to which reference is here made, who will not grant that scientific theories have been assailed with undue severity, and quite needless apprehension, under the influence of religious zeal. On the other hand, it is equally beyond dispute that there has been in some scientific quarters an eagerness to interpret scientific theories in a manner adverse to theological belief, and often with undisguised pleasure in the task, as if some real gain to thought and practical interests were to be secured by injury to religion. The best work on both sides has been done quite apart from these outbreaks of antagonism. But it would be unwise to omit reference to them here, or to overlook the lesson they convey, all the more that both sides admit reasonable ground for regret. There has been, on the one hand, too great readiness in charging an atheistic conclusion as the logical result of scientific theory; and, on the other, too hasty an assumption that newly recognized facts must prove damaging to Christian faith. Detailed illustration would be in every sense undesirable here, but outstanding examples will readily occur. Take the theory of the Development of Species by Natural Selection, to which detailed reference will be made hereafter, which has a great multitude of facts to favor it, and at the same time a mass of facts presenting most serious logical difficulties; it is obvious that even if this theory were accepted in the form in which it is at present propounded, not only would the rational basis for belief in the Divine existence and government not be affected by it, but the demand on a Sovereign Intelligence would be intensified. The contrast in the form of the general question may be represented thus: in the one case, to account for the origin of varied forms of life entirely distinct and independent; in the other, to account for an origin in the simplest germinal form, or in a few primordial forms, which shall nevertheless provide for the appearance of all the varieties of species of animal life now known to us. In presenting the latter hypothesis, science presses into notice a much greater perplexity affecting the origin of the universe, originating a difficulty towards the solution of which it is altogether unable to offer the slightest contribution. In this single illustration, there is much to convince theologians and scientific men that each division of thinkers will best fulfil its own part, and most honor religion and science, by working unreservedly on data within its own reach, without apprehension as to ultimate conflict.

From the other side, it is not difficult to find evidence that continued inquiry and reflection have led to the abatement, if not the actual withdrawal, of scientific hypotheses which seemed at variance with common belief, and which might be taken as adverse to religious thought. For example, as a branch of the inquiry connected with the theory of development of species, and coming directly upon the position of man in the scale of being, we had for a time a wonderful amount of observation, description, and discussion concerning monkeys and apes. Laborious inquiries became provocative of grotesque fancy. In the train of science came the workers who minister to the popular imagination, and there appeared a whole series of comic pictures, amusing narratives, and even musical compositions, representing monkeys and apes as taking part in human occupations. These have left their testimony to the power of scientific hypothesis in determining the thought and interest of the time during which they find favor. It was demonstrated incontestably that the anatomical structure of the ape was much more like to that of man than the structure of the dog, or the horse; and that the brain of the ape was so like in form and arrangement to the human brain, that it might be represented as a smaller and undeveloped example of the human brain. But when the work of observation and description had been well nigh completed; when the work of deliberate thinking was commenced with the assurance that the facts were pretty fully and fairly before us, there came a considerable abatement for the enthusiasm of scientific speculation in the new line of discovery. Next came the acknowledgment that even with all the analogies and homologies of structure, seen and unseen, there was a vast chasm between the ape and man. Forthwith, the stimulus to comic talent began to die away; and it must be confessed that the department of anthropology has not been greatly advanced from this new region of observation.

These examples may suffice to impress at once upon theologians and scientists,—and upon the public mind also,—the obvious, but easily forgotten lesson, that there is need for deliberation before we can clearly decide the exact significance of new scientific discoveries. Neither the spirit of religion, nor the scientific spirit, disposes inquirers to make haste. There is a basis of certainty, sufficiently broad and deep to deliver the mind from concern lest intellectual confusion should arise from continued observation and thought. Enthusiasm, acuteness, patience, and also boldness of speculation, are needed in order to widen the range of our knowledge of the mysteries of existence; but caution is as certainly a necessary feature in the gathering of appliances which must lie at the command of theologians and also of scientific observers. In fact, there is at every fresh advance in science, much *thinking* to be done, after observation and exposition have accomplished their part, and this thinking can not be quickly done.

Towards a clear marking out of the boundaries of science and religion, it is needful that some definition or description of both be attempted. It is easy to be religious without sharply marking off for one's self the exact boundaries of religion; and equally easy to be scientific, without exactly laying down the limits of science. But any intelligent view of the relations of the two is not to be had without carefully marking off the territory which they respectively occupy. Science at least should seek for itself "a scientific boundary," and though this is not always easily found, it is essential for keeping up friendly relations with neighboring states. In view, therefore, of the requirements of the present subject, something must here be done in the way of definition, or at least, description, delicate and difficult as is the task.

The object of these lectures is, to vindicate the place of the Christian religion within the region of human intelligence, to show its rational harmony with science, and to promote active co-operation between the two. And this is to be done for the Christian religion in view of all the advantages, and of all the alleged disadvantages too, of what has been reproachfully named "a book religion," which assuredly it is, just as all science must become "book science," if it is to become a living and abiding intellectual power among men. For all reliable knowledge must be formulated, must take a definite orderly shape, if it is to find a place and dominion. In the history of intelligent being in this world, religion first of all met this requirement, and subjected itself to this test, adapting itself also to successive ages, and submitting itself to their criticism. Science owns a like intellectual necessity, and has had to write and rewrite, to correct and expand, in order that the book-science might be the true science of the day. Whatever be the nature of the truth received by man, its statement is greatly enhanced in value when it has been reduced to written form, suitable not only for being passed from hand to hand, but for being pondered with all deliberation.

While, however, it is a great advantage to Christianity that it can be described as the religion of the Bible,—and it is to Christianity that reference is directly made here when religion is named,—there is in religion as in science that which comes before the written form. Observation and reflection are natural avenues to religion, as well as to science. The Bible appeals to the intelligence of man for its acceptance, subjecting to rational test not only its evidence but also its teaching. Its uniform demand is that men put its teaching to proof. It thus presupposes a natural religion as the prerequisite for special revelation of the supernatural. The full breadth of the argument in exposition and defence of Christianity is seen only by starting from this position, that all religion, whatever its form, rests on a rational basis. And its correlative is this, irreligion is the irrational. The vindication of the Christian religion thus implies at its basis the defence of religious thought and feeling in whatever associations they may be found. For though it is true that the Christian religion may be said to war against all religions besides, seeking to supplant them, in order to become the universal religion, it does so only on the footing that religious thought and feeling wherever found have a genuine intellectual value, which must work towards deliverance from what is immoral and what is inconsistent in tradition. If it be here remarked that science also tends to the destruction of the traditional beliefs belonging to many of the religions of the world, it may thereby appear that science becomes a fellow-worker with Christianity in a process of demolition required in the interests equally of intelligence, morality, and religion. But whatever may be said of this destructive process as one in which Christianity performs a conspicuous part, the religion of Jesus recognizes a voice in the works of creation speaking to the hearts of men, in all lands, insomuch that "there is no speech nor language where their voice is not heard." Religious belief is thus recognized as a natural possession, and reverence for the Most High as following by rational sequence.

When therefore we offer a defence of the Christian faith and practice, we necessarily undertake some defence of the varied manifestations of natural religion presenting themselves in the world's history. We are not precluded from assigning value to the loftier and purer thought of ancient civilization testifying against "the gods many and lords many" of the popular religion; nor do we refuse to make acknowledgment of those ruder and baser examples of religious observance appearing among tribes of uncivilized men in modern times. In defending religion, we are upholding the lofty conceptions of the Greek philosopher, who said that "God is not the author of evil, but of good only;" who declared that God "is one and the same, immutably fixed in his own proper nature," and that "God and his attributes are absolutely perfect." * On the other hand, we can not escape the serious entanglement found among heathen idolatries, for even while such idolatries are utterly condemned, we are ready to maintain that the most irrational idolatries have more of reason in them than the life which has been emptied of religious faith and exercise.

In view of the wide range of natural religion, and the defence of it here implied, we may define religion, as the recognition of a Sovereign Intelligence originating and gov-

* Plato's *Republic* II. 380, 381.

erning all dependent being, with the homage due from intelligent beings to the Sovereign Intelligence. This is the definition which will include all natural religion, and present the ground of its defence in view of scientific suggestions and perplexities.

But taking the Christian religion as the crown and centre of religious life in the world, we have a more full and commanding testimony as to the glory of the divine nature, and the genuine exercises of a religious life. He is God creating and sustaining all, ruling in righteousness, revealing himself in Jesus Christ, whose glory is "the glory as of the only begotten of the Father full of grace and truth." He is a God seeking the reconciliation of the guilty with himself. He is a God of mercy, calling all intelligent creatures to fellowship with him, and requiring them all to be "holy even as he is holy." Such is a summary of the teaching of Scripture as to the Divine Being, and our relation to him. Thus are we guided in our utterance before him, "O Lord of hosts, God of Israel, that dwellest between the cherubim, thou art the God, even thou alone, of all the kingdoms of the earth: thou hast made heaven and earth" (Isa. xxxvii. 16).

I content myself with a mere summary; for a full knowledge we must take the Bible itself, knowledge of which must be presumed as the condition of criticism, though criticism has been abundant which has borne witness to ignorance of the revelation criticised,—ignorance so marked that had it applied to science it would have been held a proof of incompetence for criticism. We are now to take the Bible representation of God, and of his relation to us; and on the other hand of man's faith in him, and spiritual devotion and service. These are the materials to be harmonized with the teachings of science, by demonstrating that the testimony of science points to a government of the universe harmonizing with the testimony of Scripture. And here it is needful that there be explicitness, that our thesis may be placed beyond doubt. The purpose is not merely to show that science lays no foundation for denial of a Supreme Intelligence, or for an atheistic conception of the universe; nor merely that it affords no place for belief in Deity without knowledge of his nature, for utterance of an empty name, without intelligible content, or an agnosticism, which affects to celebrate the praises of Ignorance, in homage to the name of science; nor merely an immanent or indwelling Deity, who is in all things, and all things in him, so that he is the unifying power, the soul and life of all that is, including those strange contrasts which we call good and evil; but passing all these representations as strange and alien to the Bible, to show that religion and science find their harmony in recognition of a Transcendent Deity, a personal Deity, distinct from the universe,—a personality ruling in righteousness, and delighting to meet the desires of intelligent beings longing after the perfection of holiness.

I can imagine that some devoted students of science are prepared to object to having any share in a discussion which is to include as one of its terms such a purely spiritual conception as this, involving a spiritual relation,—and having as its practical expression a spiritual life.

Not a few scientific men may be prepared to say that all this is quite remote from the region with which they are familiar,—that science can hardly be said to come into contact with such a spiritual region of inquiry. And I grant that there is reason for urging such a consideration. Science can not occupy the place of religion, any more than religion can occupy the place of science. But if there be any on that account feeling themselves precluded from entering on the discussion, they do thereby proclaim themselves disqualified for making any affirmation as to conflict between the two courses of thought and interest. The logical fairness of this argument admits of no challenge. Either scientists must refrain from assertions of conflict,—or they must take the declarations of the Bible, and prove their antagonism to the teachings of science, recognized as belonging to a different sphere of inquiry. As well propose to criticise the conclusions of astronomy in disregard of spectrum analysis, as propose to criticise the intellectual worth of religion in neglect of its spiritual significance.

I next pass over to inquire what Science is, taking its own testimony concerning its province and purpose, as I have taken the testimony of religion. Science has for its sphere or province the whole field of outward observation; and has for its purpose the explanation of facts within this field, either by means of direct observations as to the relations of things, or by logical inference from such observations. This field of study is full of interest, and practically inexhaustible. The trustworthiness of the method admits of no doubt, whether we consider direct observation, or guarded and careful inference from things observed. To trust our powers of observation, and to rely on our reasoning faculty, are the fundamental conditions of all knowledge. Through these avenues religious knowledge must come, as well as scientific. The risk of conflict is thus excluded here. Nor will any one dispute the inherent value of scientific knowledge.* Least of all could such a challenge come from a religious basis, for the book of nature is to the religious mind the revelation of God in its own place and form, just as the Bible is in a different and higher form. The reverence belonging to religion will not derogate from the dignity of science. The natural and genuine tendency of religious thought must be to exalt science, in its proper sense, as a verified explanation of the facts of existence. A contrary tendency can arise only in one of two ways, either when religion is driven back on the defensive on account of scientific theory

* See Appendix I.

assuming an attitude of antagonism; or when religious thought has been contracted into narrow and hardened form, such as to encourage isolation from regions of investigation personally disliked. In the one case, dishonor is reflected on scientific thinking, in the other, dishonor is cast on religious thought.

These considerations will indicate the true intellectual spirit in which we should face the question concerning the relations of religion and science. To our rational nature, every thing which is entitled to rank as genuine knowledge must be matter of interest; and reliance on common means of acquiring knowledge, must involve confidence in the unity of all truth, and the possibility of demonstrating such unity, if only it be possible for us to penetrate deep enough, and extend our researches wide enough,—a confidence which will not be sacrificed even when the actual unity waits discovery. As each one of the planets diffuses its own share of light, and all combine to constitute the solar system, so each science must be a centre of knowledge, and all combined must constitute a system of truth.

This being granted on purely intellectual

grounds, our concluding point is connected with competency to enter upon critical inquiry as to the harmony of religion and science. What has been said as to knowledge of the Bible as a prerequisite for the discussion of our problem, must equally hold as to science. One thing, however, needs to be fairly stated and deliberately allowed; the possibility of intelligent and adequate criticism does not imply full acquaintance with scientific methods, and personal ability to test the results of their application. Most of us must be content to take our scientific knowledge on trust, as Chaucer did, when he declined to enter upon the intricacies of astronomical study, because he was too old for making satisfactory progress.* To accept scientific conclusions without personal verification is simply inevitable. When scientific men themselves have come to a general agreement, and are not any longer in conflict on a particular conclusion, this must be enough for the great majority of intelligent inquirers.

* "'Wilt thou learne of sterres ought?'
'Nay, certainly,' quod I, 'right naught.'
'And why?' quod he. 'For I am old.'"
House of Fame, B. II, 487.

There is not, in this, absolute security for accuracy, but neither is there such security in the circumstances for scientific men themselves, and there can be no reasonable ground for hesitancy or complaint, either on our part or on theirs, if we are ready to accept general agreement as sufficient testimony for the time. It would be utterly impracticable and unreasoning to insist that we can not intelligently accept the conclusions of astronomy unless we are able to go through the mathematical processes; or the main facts of human physiology unless we have verified each position by personal investigation into the structure of the organs, and the conditions of functional activity. Conjectures find from an intelligent public no higher acknowledgment than is due to conjecture, simply because those who have devoted themselves to research in the department concerned are not agreed in attributing to them any higher significance. On the other hand, conclusions are accepted as true, however much they may be at variance with previously existing conviction, when the great majority of scientific inquirers have admitted the observations to be undoubted or the reasonings conclusive. This is the only conceivable test. It is that which scientific thinkers must themselves recognize as the rule of credence in all departments of investigation lying beyond their own familiar field of study; and it is that which is naturally accepted by the whole body of non-scientific readers and thinkers interested in the advance of knowledge. All practiced theologians, and all upholders of religion on the ground of intelligent warrant for belief and practice, only take the ground of common intelligence when they accept implicitly the conclusions reached by scientific procedure.

Whatever then may be the evidence of conflict between science and religion, and whatever the difficulties lying in the way of working out reconciliation, there is clear warrant for claiming common ground from which to start, and that so ample and secure that it is provided by scientific inquiry itself, and generally accepted by educated men of all classes. There can be no patchwork contrivance, made up of what may be taken to be final statements of theological and scientific positions. We do not aim at some agglomeration of materials gathered from opposite quarters and brought together with the design of constructing a compact and durable unity. Neither from the side of religion, nor from that of science, could such a proposal find countenance. Each must work from its own basis, the one from Revelation, the other from Nature. Each must go on its own course of development and active service, unaided and undeterred by the other. And from age to age in the world's progress it must continue part of the task connected with intelligent existence, to go from one to the other, in search of the lines of harmony. From both sides must come an impulse to this search for agreement. From the scientific side, by an intellectual necessity, for all intelligent research presses on towards unity in a complete conquest of the region of investigation, pushing out in distinct lines with full conviction of the harmony of being, and of conclusions expressing so much of this harmony as has been definitely ascertained. And what is no less certain, though not so freely admitted, all investigation as to the laws of existence, even that which proclaims confidence only in observation, with inference from what it discloses, is urging the human mind onward to a higher range of questions as to existence beyond observation, and the causes of things visible. Impotent in the extreme has been the voice of a "positive" philosophy, denouncing the search for causes, sounding its trumpet call to rally all divisions of scientific workers to search exclusively for facts, as if such workers were but a band of quarrymen, boring, blasting, and gathering up shattered fragments of rock. For facts must science ever search; with nothing short of ascertained facts can it be satisfied; but, having found them, it must classify and harmonize, seeking for the laws which regulate their occurrence, and for the causes by which they may be rationally explained.

On the other hand, from the sphere of religion must ever arise a powerful impulse to seek harmony of conviction with the verified results of scientific research. This may be expected to prove a more urgent and practical necessity than that which operates from within the region of science. The belief in a personal Deity, as the source of all dependent existence, and the controller of all, leads by a necessity both intellectual and spiritual to a search for order in all things, and a harmony of the universe. Viewed only as an intellectual discipline,—and this is an important though partial view of it,—religion develops what may be described as the intellectual instinct, craving for knowledge, with expectation of order and harmony everywhere, and with prospect of ample reward for patient research. Religion, beginning with the conception of a transcendent Being,—seeing in finite existence a creation and a cosmos,—gives more powerful stimulus to search for harmony of truth, than can be said to spring from science. The latter by the necessity of its procedure begins by contracting thought in order to concentrate, and is apt to encourage its most devoted servants to work on isolated divisions of existence, relegating to a distant future the greater and more puzzling task of contemplating the harmony of all sciences. It is, then, by pressing into view an urgent practical and personal need, that religion may be said in the history of individual life to contribute the strongest motive power towards such intellectual effort as is concerned with the harmonizing of all truth. This will appear in personal experience according to the intellectual activity of the individual, under the requirements of his religious life, and in study of all that belongs to the system of the universe. This being recognized and avowed, as following from the very nature of religion, it devolves on the Church in all its divisions,—the brotherhood of believers,—to manifest a genuine and profound interest in the progress of science, making felt in the world the full influence of the spirit, at once scientific and religious, which seeks to discover and demonstrate the harmony of created existence.

LECTURE II.

EXPERIENCE GATHERED FROM PAST CONFLICTS.

THERE have been within quite recent times conflicts as to the relations of science and religion, which have now lost their living interest. All classes greatly affected by current literature, and scientific discussion, whether ranking themselves on the side of religion, or otherwise, were deeply moved by them. It appeared at the time, as if some new position were to be marked off, destined to affect our whole conception of the government of the universe. The expectation was not verified; public interest died away; and preparations for conflict were abandoned, on account of the unexpected discovery that there was nothing to fight about.

It is a wise rule affecting our busy life, crowded with present-day duties, that we allow subjects quietly to drop out of view which have lost living interest. But this wise rule is turned to unwise ends, if it make us forgetful of the lessons of the past. Scientific progress consists in the abandonment of untenable positions, for occupancy of others proved to be more reliable. Accordingly the conflict which seems to threaten the interests of religion wears now one aspect and now another, as determined by the stage of scientific progress which has been reached. But all intellectual progress is an evolution, bearing at every moment some trace of what has been left behind, as well as evidence of accretion. A large amount of the experience connected with intellectual life is gathered from events connected with abandoning positions of past interest, as well as from those associated with what is new. I propose, therefore, though within comparatively narrow limits, to refer to past conflicts, quite recent, but practically at an end. The ebb and flow of intellectual interests follow in such rapid succession, and each is so absorbing during its continuance, that we readily forget the tangled waste buried from sight under the spring-tide of rising expectation. We easily lose sight of the past, even though it lie close at hand, and as we feel the pulse of life beat high in proportion to the vividness and apparent value of our prospects, we are ever liable to overestimate the importance of the present position, thus severing ourselves too readily from all that lies behind. There may be reason for cutting down bridges in the rear, if there be apprehension of cowardice in the ranks; but where the calmness and courage of resolute progress are found, there is no need for a yawning chasm behind. It is true, indeed, that just beyond some bridges recently crossed, there lie a good many traces of humiliation. And it is according to the tendency of human nature, whether religious or anti-religious, to turn away from that which occasions uneasiness. But there is a moral, as well as an intellectual demand, for thoroughness in recognizing the continuity of events. The scientific spirit can not excuse a covering up of past failures, as the formulating of verified results must imply testimony concerning them. It is of the very nature of religious conviction that we should learn from the failures of the past, and should advance out of them with higher wisdom. By common consent, therefore, we can have no accurate survey of the present situation, without making account of what has been recently passed, as well as what may be regarded as pressing upon our notice in these days.

We do not need to travel a long way to the rear in order to discover how far astray we may be, both in expectations and in apprehensions; how readily we may get into confusion as to the interests involved in exciting controversies; and how much we need caution, making allowance for our partial survey of facts, and our uncertainty as to what may open up.

By way of illustration, I shall refer to the history of discussions concerning so-called "*spontaneous generation*," mixed up with ascertained facts as to protoplasm, bathybius, or "living slime," as it has been called, and bacterium. The question eagerly discussed was whether there might be origin of life, without development from germ, seed, or ovum. The problem was one of those suggestions apt to arise under pressure of new conjectures and theories. While the scientific world was astir on the question of development, attention was turned for a time towards the possibility of a fresh beginning of organic forms, life which should be no development, but should rather seem as an uncaused existence,—"spontaneous generation." It might have been urged that the suggestion was contrary to reason; that "inexorable logic," of which we often hear from scientific observers, forbade the supposition; that all the conditions of scientific thought were against it; that the very conception of "spontaneous generation" was a logical inconsistency, alien to the requirements of scientific thought, as implying uncaused existence; but we were reminded that we are prohibited from supposing any thing is impossible in the pathway of science, that observation must be first, and reason only second, and accordingly the needful experiments went on under all due precautions. The brief chapter in the history of science which records expectations and results connected with these experiments, well deserves to be remembered. It is here selected for illustration, both on account of its inherent importance, and its relation to the theory of development, which must afterwards have special attention.

Some descent is required from ordinary scientific observation to the level where this question is discussed. From the germ-cell, we pass down to an albuminous substance spread over the ocean-bed, said to have life, or we descend to microscopic organisms, such as bacteria; and a step lower down still, we are introduced to the question whether in water passed through the boiling process so as to guard against the presence of germinal forms, we may not witness the origin of life.

The question so raised had additional interest because of the bearing it might have on the first appearance of life in the history of this world. This interest was shared on both sides, by those who held that creation is a conception not only alien to scientific thought (which it may well be*), but inconsistent with it; and by those who regarded creation as the only conception adequate to meet rational requirements. The question had at the same time a direct practical interest connected with public health, on account of its bearing upon the diffusion and vital tenacity of spores or germinal forms capable of spreading contagious disease.†

* Science can not reach the beginning of things.

† See *Disease Germs, their Nature and Origin*, by Beale. London, Churchill; Philadelphia, Lindsay and Blaikiston.

The controversy on this subject was at its height in the years 1876, and 1877, having a large amount of most careful and difficult experiment devoted to it. The result has been a valuable addition to scientific knowledge as to the vitality of germinal forms, and a quietus to theories as to "spontaneous generation."

The direct object placed before the scientific mind when the discussion arose was this, —to ascertain whether an origin of vital activity could be observed in the midst of materials from which all germinal forms of life were certainly excluded.

The selection of materials to experiment upon was for a time according to the fancy of the experimenter. It was not proposed that a vacuum should be made by withdrawal of all air from a glass vessel, thereafter watching for the appearance of some organic form. Nor was it suggested that pure water might be taken from a spring, and boiled, and left standing under daily observation. A great variety of materials was selected to provide an infusion which might afford the conditions for application of scientific tests. In this way the following materials were used and tested, infusion of turnip, of pounded cheese, hay, meat, fish, besides egg-albumen, blood, and urine. Vegetable productions, animal tissue, and secretions of the human body closely connected with vital processes, were thus subjected to test. In the history of investigation, attention ultimately concentrated on the infusion of hay and on urine. Observations were conducted in Paris and London; results were published from time to time; singular divergence became apparent in these recorded results; this led to controversy, which became so keen, that the Academy of Sciences in Paris appointed a commission of three to adjudicate upon a challenge given by M. Pasteur of Paris to Dr. Bastian of London; which Commission met in Paris on 15th July, 1877, but never adjudicated in the matter.*

The perplexities encountered in conducting observations arose chiefly from two causes: the difficulty of ascertaining the temperature at which living organisms were certainly destroyed, and the materials sterilized; and that of guarding against interference with this state when established, by contact with the atmosphere. The latter perplexity, involving much care, skilful manipulation, and mechanical con-

* *Nature* vol. xvi. p. 276.

trivance, was at last overcome by the construction of glass tubes, separating for a time the distinct materials, with facility for their mixture at the proper moment without contact with the air.

The true scientific difficulty, however, was determination of a reliable test for destruction of germinal forms, either adhering to the materials, embedded in them, or floating in the atmosphere. The history of observations bearing on this question is deeply interesting. In the earlier tentative experiments, the material placed under observation was boiled; it was concluded that no vital organism could endure this process; and the material was kept for a time in a temperature of from seventy to eighty degrees Fahr., which was regarded as favorable to the development of life. In process of time, a deposit appeared in the tube, and this when examined under the microscope was found to contain bacteria,* living, moving germinal forms so minute as to require high magnifying power for their discovery. Here then was "spontaneous generation." Who could be so credulous as to

* Examples of the bacteria magnified 1,800, 3,000, and 5,000 times are given in Plate I. p. 16, of Beale's *Disease Germs*.

believe that minute organic forms could live through the boiling process? If this appeared too absurd to fancy, then spontaneous generation, or actual origin of life out of non-organized matter, must be held to be established. It was only the audacity of prejudice, and hopeless alienation from the "advanced thought" of the time, which could induce any one to doubt, in face of these experiments, carefully recorded and published.* Scientific observers of great experience and reputation felt it needful to express themselves with caution, leaving results to be tested.

A considerable number of investigators began to turn their attention to the subject, and a period of seven years was occupied before the results became so certain as to be practically final. Pasteur, Pouchet, and Joubert were at work in France, Crookes, Child, Beale, Roberts, Bastian, Tyndall and others in England.

All experiments concentrated upon certainty in sterilizing the substance operated upon. Pasteur pointed out that the chemical properties of the infusion affected the

* For Dr. Bastian's experiments see *Times*, April 13, 1870; and *Nature*, June and July, 1870.

vitality of the microscopic germs inclosed in it; and Roberts at a later stage confirmed this by independent investigation, proving "that slightly alkaline liquids are more difficult to sterilize by heat than slightly acid liquids.* In this way, it was shown that distinct records of temperature were needful, greater intensity of heat being required in some cases than in others, in order to secure destruction of germs. The facts were illustrated by hay infusion, "the acid infusion invariably remaining barren after a few minutes' boiling, and the neutralized infusion invariably becoming fertile after a similar boiling." † The neutralizing element was liquor potassæ, and the next question started was this, Did the liquor potassæ enable the germs to live longer under the boiling process, or did its infusion operate so as to originate life where germs no longer had any existence? A contrivance was adopted by which the boiling could be applied to the hay infusion, while the liquor potassæ was kept enclosed in another part of the tube, ready to be added

* Contribution to Royal Society of London. *Nature* xv. p. 302, Feb. 1, 1877.

† *Ib.*

without exposure to the air, after the boiling process was over. When added in this way, "the liquor potassæ had not any power to excite germination:" the expectation that a certain mixture of acid and alkali would originate life was disappointed; all the earlier experiments were discredited. Still, some clung to their expressed belief, for there is a prejudice of advanced thought, as there is a prejudice of old beliefs. Tenacity of avowed opinion, with strong love of research, prolonged the inquiry, and led to more decided evidence.

The controversy was conducted by Dr. Roberts against Dr. Bastian, while all the experiments of Professor Tyndall were converging upon the same conclusions as those reached by Roberts.* That Bastian had obtained bacteria after boiling, admitted of no doubt, and he naturally clung to this fact as encouraging; others regarded it as only misleading. Bastian maintained that the alkali had a positive power of originating life, and stated one hundred and twenty-two degrees Fahr. as favorable to the appearance of life. Roberts took ten examples of sterilized urine, and twenty

* *Nature* vol. xv. p. 302, and Appendix II.

nine examples of fermentible liquids which had remained over from the earlier experiments of 1873–74, and these thirty-nine examples were subjected to careful experiment and observation. In the first ten cases, the tube was heated in oil for fifteen minutes up to two hundred and eighty degrees Fahr.; the ten tubes were then set in a warm place (from seventy degrees to eighty degrees Fahr.) for a fortnight; the contents were transparent; the alkali was then allowed to mingle with it, and the tubes were placed in an incubator kept at a temperature of one hundred and fifteen degrees Fahr.; at the end of two days there was a sediment, and the liquor was clear; the tubes were replaced in the incubator, the temperature being raised to one hundred and twenty-two degrees Fahr. as recommended by Dr. Bastian; there they continued for three days; they were then withdrawn and placed under the microscope, but no trace of living organism was found either in the fluid or in the deposit under it. The twenty-nine cases, including a variety of vegetable and animal preparations were next treated in like manner, and with like results. Tyndall's experiments were reported to the Royal Society of London at the same time, with exactly the same result. M. Pasteur had previously reported to the Academy of Sciences in Paris to the same effect. It was thus proved by a mass of evidence that if proper precautions were taken to destroy germinal forms, no mixture of alkali with acid, whatever the variety of materials selected, was adequate to produce life.

A few months later than the communications of Roberts and Tyndall, that is, May, 1877, the results of ten years' experiment, first by Mr. Dallinger himself, and thereafter by Mr. Dallinger and Mr. Drysdale conjointly, were communicated to the Royal Institution, London, on "the origin and development of minute and lowly life forms.*" The purpose of these experiments was to watch the growth of the minutest germs, capable of being seen only under a powerful microscope, putting to actual test their tenacity of life. The largest objects were one-thousandth of an inch, the smallest, the four-thousandth of an inch. Six distinct forms were selected for observation, and their history was made out. A magnifying power of five thousand degrees was used. In the glairy fluid a monad larger than usual

* *Nature* vol. xvi. p. 24.

seized on a smaller; they became fused after swimming about together; the single object then appeared a motionless spec; this proved to be a sac, from which at the close of a period varying from ten to thirty-six hours, it burst, and young spores became visible in the fluid, which were kept under observation till they reached maturity. Special interest was connected with these observations not only as illustrating the growth of spores, or germs; but as allowing application of the test of heat at different stages of growth. When this test was applied, it was found that one hundred and forty degrees Fahr. was sufficient to cause the death of adults, whereas the young spores were able to live notwithstanding the application of three hundred degrees Fahr. for ten minutes. In this direction fresh discovery was to be made.

In June 1877,—a month later,—Professor Tyndall gave the record of further researches.* These presented additional results as to degrees of temperature requisite for destroying microscopic organisms. It had been already shown that alkaline liquids are more difficult to sterilize, than acid liquids; it was further

* *Nature* vol. xvi. p. 127.

shown that the death point was higher in air, than in water; for Professor Tyndall extended his researches to air, as well as liquid. First dealing with the fluid form, he found germs possessed of vitality so singular that five or six hours of boiling did not destroy them, and in one case eight hours was insufficient for the purpose. In this connection, he came to the conclusion that some germinal orders were more easily destroyed than others.

When dealing with bacteria, he found that they differed from other forms in this, that they rose to the air as if it were a requisite, whereas other germs, such as those belonging to the process of fermentation, could exist without oxygen. This led to an additional form of experiment, with the view of deciding whether bacteria could be destroyed by withdrawal of air; and if so, whether the bacteria would reappear after the existing microscopic life had been stifled. Tyndall began by applying the air-pump. Under this process the bacteria were enfeebled greatly, but not destroyed. Thereafter Sprengel pumps were used, by means of which the air dissolved in the infusions was withdrawn, as well as that diffused in the spaces above. In numerous cases there was success in destroying the germs by removal of the air in this way without any boiling process. In these cases, the air was carefully restored, precautions being adopted to guard against admission of germinal forms, and in no case did life reappear in the infusions. As in the more common style of experiment, the warmth suitable could not charm the life back again; so in this, the restoration of oxygen, could not secure restoration of life.

Thus evidence from all sides directed surely to the conclusion that the alleged discovery of "spontaneous generation" was a delusion, the result of hasty and insufficient experiment. Dr. Bastian, nevertheless, stuck heroically to his original position, and came into conflict with M. Pasteur of Paris, by means of a communication which the English Professor had sent to the Academy of Sciences in July of the previous year, 1876. In the beginning of 1877, M. Pasteur threw down an explicit challenge to Professor Bastian, which resulted in the appointment of a commission to observe the experiments and adjudicate. With this terminates the history of nearly ten years of curious and singular investigation, and Dr. Bastian himself has supplied the history of the closing scene, laying open the whole correspondence to public investigation, as if he were unconscious of the complete demolition of his favorite theory of "spontaneous generation." The 15th of July, 1877, witnessed the close of a battle he had been fighting against steadily increasing odds, and which he had begun in June, 1870. Dr. Bastian's position was "that a solution of boiled potash caused bacteria to appear in sterile urine at fifty degrees Cent., added in a quantity sufficient to neutralize the latter." These he regarded as the physico-chemical conditions for spontaneous generation of bacteria.

The challenge from M. Pasteur was in these terms;—"I defy Dr. Bastian to obtain, in the presence of competent judges, the result to which I have referred with sterile urine, on the sole condition that the solution of potash which he employs be pure, *i. e.*, made with pure water and pure potash, both free from organic matter. If Dr. Bastian wishes to use a solution of impure potash, I freely authorize him to take any in the English or any other Pharmacopœia, being diluted or concentrated, on the sole condition that that solution shall be raised beforehand to one hundred and ten degrees for twenty minutes, or to one hundred and thirty degrees for five minutes."

A Commission was appointed by the Academy, and Dr. Bastian agreed to appear before it, but only on conditions he laid down greatly restricting the range of inquiry. He ignored the first and most searching form of M. Pasteur's challenge; claimed that the adjudication of the Commission should be only on the second; and further stated that if the Commission were "to express an opinion upon the interpretation of the fact attested, and upon its bearings on 'the germ theory of fermentation,' or 'spontaneous generation,'" he would respectfully decline to take part in this wider inquiry. The Commission refused to be restricted to the worst form of the experiment, and to be bound to withhold an opinion as to its bearing on the question of "spontaneous generation." Dr. Bastian went to Paris, but the members of the Commission declined to deal with less than the challenge given, and the meeting was never properly constituted. "Thus ended," as Dr. Bastian has said, "the proceedings of this remarkable Commission of the French Academy." The proceedings ended before they had begun. Dr. Bastian by his restrictions, surrendered the real question at issue, and practically acknowledged that he would not submit it to the judgment of the Commission. He sought only testimony as to his own form of experiment, which there was then good reason to know was accurate, because M. Pasteur had stated a temperature too low, and a time too short, but which was at the same time an experiment of no scientific value for establishing "spontaneous generation." Thus ended a battle which had been protracted long after it was to all observers manifestly lost.

The discussion thus narrated may be easily overestimated, but there seems even more risk that the manifest failure should lead to an oversight of the value of the protracted investigations. These convey lessons of special value to scientific inquirers on the one hand, and to theologians on the other. They are of great value for illustrative purposes in such a course of lectures as the present, and that because they provide needful training for intelligent observation of the advance of science.

The promulgation of the development theory of species has given a conception of the unity of organic life in the world, which even in its most modified form has an imposing grandeur. Influenced by this, scientific men are naturally concerned to make out, if possible, some connection between inorganic and organic being. To work at this, is part of the inevitable task of science, even though the result should be only to establish the helplessness of science in dealing with it.

We have chemical and dynamical theories of life which stimulate repetition of experiments, in the hope that some grand discovery may be made. Those just described present a curious illustration. In the circumstances, we can well understand the persistence with which Dr. Bastian clung to his supposed discovery of the physico-chemical conditions for production of living organism.

Science finds in these experiments a fresh lesson of the need for caution, guarding against the hampering influence of popular notions, as in reference to the probable effects of the boiling process. For if the experiments have proved a failure so far as support to a theory of spontaneous generation is concerned, they have revealed a tenacity of life belonging to the lowest microscopic organisms, far beyond higher organic forms, and the consequent weakness of ordinary human devices in struggling against the development of such germs. These experiments also emphasize the need for attention to the laws of rational procedure, as well as to skill in experimental observation, if science is to be exempted from needless toils.

Theology has here also a lesson of patience, for it may well leave science to do its own work, undisturbed by apprehensions as to possible consequences to morality and religion. All that the telescope can reveal, and the microscope can make known, through years of experimenting, we wish to have discovered, for only thus shall we come to understand the world's lessons of wisdom and power lying far beyond the range of our unaided vision. All the churches of Christ have reason to hail the extension of scientific knowledge. Those who set high account on patient interpretation of the written Revelation, have reason to value this laborious reading out of the lessons written in the book of Nature.

A wider and more general result may be expected than that which bears directly on the relations of science and religion. All intelligent readers of scientific discussions will find discipline from pondering these experiments. They illustrate the toil connected with scientific research, the risks which beset such inquiry, and the limits of scientific investigations. There lies in these experiments a warning of the constant need for falling back not only on the laws of evidence, but also on the laws of reason. The mere conception of "spontaneous generation," rigidly interpreted, were a curiosity, coming wonderfully near a contradiction of scientific thought itself, which seeks for causes, and repudiates uncaused occurrences. There may naturally enough be a discovery of the chemical elements belonging to definite types of organism, or of the form and measure of energy operating in life. Even when surmising "that possibly we may by the help of physical principles, especially that of the dissipation of energy, sometime attain to a notion of what constitutes life, mere vitality, nothing higher," Professor Tait has thought it needful to add, "but let no one imagine that, should we ever penetrate this mystery, we shall thereby be enabled to produce, except from life, even the lowest form of life."* If it were suggested that physico-chemical elements could originate life, chemistry would easily supply the ingredients. If it were hinted that reliance might be placed exclusively on the action of air or of heat for producing living organism from inorganic matter, this were to fall back on the old elemental philosophy of ancient Greece, which the thought of Greece easily repudiated without the aid of experimental science.

Attention is, however, here concentrated on the failure of these experiments meant to establish "spontaneous generation," and in this failure we find illustration of the fact that supposed conflicts between science and religion are often misunderstandings and nothing more, based on unreliable experiments or unwarranted expectations.

One other fact deserves to be recorded and placed in companionship with that just stated, that some of the alleged conflicts between science and religion are delusively so described, on account of misunderstanding or misrepresentation of religion. They are fictitious articles, requiring to be properly branded, and quietly laid aside. A single illustration may

* *Recent Advances in Physical Science*, p. 24.

suffice, taken from Dr. Draper's *History of the Conflict between Religion and Science*, which is easily accessible, and reasonably claims some attention in connection with the present subject. The criticism here offered is not meant to carry a general condemnation of the book. This work includes a vast deal more than its title suggests; in the midst of much that is extraneous, there is not a little of valuable historical matter written in a clear and attractive style. The book is, however, in many parts misleading, often by its style suggesting that the author has allowed himself to be carried away in his eagerness to make out serious conflict. The plan of the book is hardly compatible with fairness. This may be illustrated by reference to the grounds for selecting illustrations of Christianity. Our author says, "In speaking of Christianity reference is generally made to the Roman Church, partly because its adherents compose the majority of Christendom, partly because its demands are the most pretentious, and partly because it has commonly sought to enforce those demands by the civil power."* In view of these explanations, it may be in a

* *Preface* x.

sense satisfactory, as suggesting more harmony between science and religion than the general tenor of the book conveys, that Professor Draper has "had little to say" respecting the Protestant and Greek Churches. But the reasons for making the Roman division of the Church representative of the whole are far from satisfactory. It is as if one were bent on fighting, but determined always to select the weakest antagonist to be found. Nor is the case improved by the defence offered. Dr. Draper says, "In thus treating the subject, it has not been necessary to pay much regard to more moderate or intermediate opinions, for, though they may be intrinsically of great value, in conflicts of this kind it is not with the moderates, but with the extremists, that the impartial reader is mainly concerned. Their movements determine the issue."* This is, I think, an unwise conclusion. Extremists may determine the erratic deflections of a movement; they do not decide its issues. They discover the heat, rather than the thought, involved in intellectual conflict. They contribute to vortex movement, rather than onward.

In consequence of his plan of procedure,

* *Preface* x.

Dr. Draper gives often a misleading view of the relative positions of religion and science. A reference to Chapter VI. will afford illustration. The subject is, "Conflict Respecting the Nature of the World." The two prominent contrasts placed at the head of this chapter are these:—"Scriptural view of the world; the earth a flat surface: scientific view; the earth a globe." These are, indeed, complete contrasts; but the question is, Are they accurately stated? Is there any warrant for saying that Scripture teaches that the earth is a flat surface? Most Bible readers of the present day will take this as quite a discovery. That there was long and earnest discussion of the question whether the earth was flat or a globe, is certain. But it is erroneous to refer to Scripture as the source of the former position. The opening of the chapter sufficiently disposes of the suggestion. Dr. Draper says, —"An uncritical observation of the aspect of nature persuades us that the earth is an extended level surface which sustains the dome of the sky, a firmament dividing the waters above from the waters beneath; that the heavenly bodies—the sun, the moon, the stars—pursue their way moving from east to west, their insignificant size, and motion round the motionless earth, proclaiming their inferiority. Of the various organic forms surrounding man none rival him in dignity, and hence he seems justified in concluding that every thing has been created for his use—the sun for the purpose of giving him light by day, the moon and stars by night. Comparative theology shows that this is the conception of nature universally adopted in the early phase of intellectual life. It is the belief of all nations in all parts of the world in the beginning of their civilization." *

In determining the relations of religion and science it is impossible to accept a passage so general, and full of mixed references as this. There is, indeed, no reason to complain of statements as to the general impressions resulting from "an uncritical observation" of nature, and of the testimony which may be drawn from "comparative theology." Such references are to be valued, as belonging to an important branch of inquiry; but they are not to be mixed up with statements concern-

* *History of the Conflict between Religion and Science*, by J. W. Draper, M.D., LL.D., Professor in the University of New York. 12 ed., p. 152.

ing Scripture teaching. Such commingling leads to confusion, and deprives a discussion of historical accuracy and scientific precision. In view of the immense practical, as well as scientific interests involved, it is needful to guard against loose statements encouraging a belief in conflict between religion and science, where no such conflict exists. The passage here selected is taken as an example, and its criticism will indicate what claims religion has a right to make upon scientific men in their management of such discussions. It may be that with equal reason a similar claim can be turned upon defenders of religion in view of their criticisms of scientific discussions. But the real value of such investigations, from whatever side they come, depends upon accurate and guarded statement. It is to be feared, however, that Dr. Draper's theory that "extremists determine the issue," may tempt him to favor a different rule.

To state that the scriptural view of the world is, that "the earth is a flat surface," is misrepresentation. And the variety of form into which this statement is thrown throughout the chapter makes it greatly worse. Thus our author speaks of "the flat figure of the earth, as revealed in the Scriptures,"* as if this quasi-scientific statement were part of Bible revelation. Again he speaks of "the theological doctrine of the flatness of the earth" being irretrievably overthrown.† Once more, where speaking of the Copernican system of astronomy, he speaks of Copernicus not only as influenced by his exposure to punishment from the Roman Church, but as being "aware that his doctrines were totally opposed to revealed truth."‡ These successive statements involve additional exaggeration.

Our author gives no references which the reader may examine for himself. There can be little doubt that he points to the exceedingly grand and impressive passage at the opening of the book of Genesis. But in that passage there is nothing to support the statement that "the flat figure of the earth" is part of Bible revelation. That the earth has been supposed flat, and that this is really taught in Scripture, are two very different things. The Bible which says, that "the earth was without form and void, and dark-

* *History of the Conflict between Religion and Science,* p. 163.
† *Ib.* p. 165. ‡ *Ib.* p. 167.

ness was upon the face of the deep," and records the will of the Supreme Ruler at a later stage in these words, "And God said let the waters under the heaven be gathered together into one place, and let the dry land appear," * does something quite the opposite of teaching that "the earth is a flat surface."

Nor do the Scriptures teach that "the earth sustains the dome of the sky." In remote times such an opinion as to the resting-place for the great dome had its supporters. But there is no pretext for attributing the teaching of this to the Bible. The scriptural statement is "God made the firmament, and divided the waters which were under the firmament from the waters which were above the firmament; and it was so. And God called the firmament Heaven." There is no reader of these words, even if he have only "an uncritical observation of the aspect of nature," who can suppose that the "firmament" here means "the dome of the sky." This statement places certain waters "*above* the firmament," and there is no one who is at once a reader of the Bible, and an observer of nature, who thinks of the clouds as above the

* Genesis i. 2, 9.

sky; but every one knows that there is an expanse which bears these water treasures far up from the earth's surface. The word rendered "firmament,"* from the Vulgate *firmamentum*, really means "expanse," and most naturally and obviously refers to the atmosphere surrounding the earth, upon which the clouds are borne aloft, and carried to and fro. Taking into account the want of scientific knowledge of the structure of the earth in far past ages, and the representations inconsistent with facts which found currency, the true marvel is that the statements of Scripture so simply and naturally harmonize with discoveries not made till the sixteenth century of the Christian era. This is a marvel which will more deeply impress us the longer it is pondered.

If we extend our consideration to the cruder notions which found acceptance in the dark ages, such as that to which Bruno referred, that the earth is a flat surface, *supported on pillars*, the scriptural evidence pled in its favor appears grotesquely inadequate. The passages are these. First stands Hannah's

* רָקִיעַ, from רָקַע, to spread out.

outburst of devotional feeling on the occasion of presenting her son Samuel before the Lord. In magnifying the greatness of God, she says, "the pillars of the earth are the Lord's, and he hath set the world upon them."* Next come the utterances of Job, when enlarging on the power of the Almighty. In one of his replies to his irritating counsellors, when speaking of the works of Jehovah, he says, "which shaketh the earth out of her place, and the pillars thereof tremble."† In another passage of similar construction, he says of God, "He hath compassed the waters with bounds, until the day and night come to an end. The pillars of heaven tremble, and are astonished at his reproof."‡ There is no Bible reader who can readily fall into such an obvious mistake as to treat these highly figurative utterances, as if they were formal revelations concerning the structure of the universe. As well might we, in reading the words of Paul concerning the position and influence of prominent disciples in the early church, in which he says that James, Cephas, and John "seemed to be pillars," proceed to deduce from this statement the revelation that the spiritual kingdom is a

* I Samuel ii. 8. † Job ix. 6. ‡ Job xxvi. 10, 11.

flat surface on which are based the pillars upholding the heavenly kingdom into which the Saviour has entered.

This short reference to the structure and relative position of the earth, will suffice to illustrate the fact that in dealing with the alleged conflicts between religion and science, it is needful to cast aside a number of manufactured difficulties, which do not arise from legitimate interpretation of Scripture. The particular criticism here introduced is adopted for a general purpose,—to lessen complications, and secure a proper understanding of the actual relation of the Bible to scientific research.

From a very early period in the history of scientific inquiry, it has been more or less clearly recognized that the Bible is not a science-revelation, but a revelation of religious truth and duty, discovering the true ideal and destiny of man in fellowship with God. Let us have it kept clear on both sides, that there is no divine revelation of scientific truth. Nature is its own revelation, and the only revelation, whose secrets must be laboriously sought out by successive generations of investigators from all of whom is required patient, persevering research, with undeviating and single love of truth. Those early inquirers who found themselves in painful contact with the persecuting power of the Roman Church, such as Galileo, and Bruno, recognized to some extent that conflict with the Church and conflict with the Bible were not exactly identical. And those of us who are clearly and resolutely on the side of religious faith and religious life, have need to ponder this lesson of history, that those defending the Bible have not always been guided by its teaching in their defence, and have not always fully apprehended the Bible teaching on the subject with which their efforts were concerned.

But what we most need in these days to keep conspicuous is the true view of the Bible as a professed revelation from God. It does not profess to be a revelation of facts such as scientific appliances are adequate to ascertain, while it does profess to discover facts both as to the universe and as to man, which science can not approach. It is not a history of the earth, but it includes within it, historical records of events closely connected with man's moral and spiritual well-being. It does not train man "to regard himself as the principal object of the care of Nature";* it does not even suggest thought in this direction, but it teaches that God cares for righteousness more than he cares for material things; that man as a being of flesh and blood is unspeakably insignificant, his life being "even a vapor that appeareth for a little time, and then vanisheth away";† that his spiritual life, in the love of God and in fellowship with him, is immeasurably great, the purpose of the Bible concerning man, as revealed by Jesus Christ, God's Son, being this, that man shall be like to God in moral purity.

From these few statements it may readily appear what is the attitude of the Bible towards science. It leaves man to his own research for the structure of science in all its divisions; it proffers no help in such work; but has a range of application quite beyond the area traversed by science.

In this way we find the natural interpretation of inevitable conflicts in the past, which have been roughly and often inaccurately described as conflicts between religion and sci-

* *Conflict between Religion and Science*, p. 172.

† James iv. 14.

ence. These conflicts were in the strictest sense inevitable, simply because thought and discovery have been progressive; and it is impossible for those not personally engaged in research to accept without reluctance new representations of familiar facts. If men long continued unwilling to admit that the earth moves round the sun, and that the rising and setting of the luminary are delusions, while the succession of light and darkness is real, we can not wonder at this slowness of assent, or charge it to the power of religious thought. The conflict was not between religion and science, but between popular notions and scientific observations. Often in the earlier periods of awakened thought, following the slumber of the middle ages, the contest accidentally wore a religious aspect, but it was so only because the higher intelligence and the general work of instruction belonged to the religious orders.

If, however, we give due weight to historical facts, it will appear that the rectification of common thought as to the form of the earth, and its place in relation to the heavenly bodies, was achieved through the conflict of a later science with an earlier. Science has first taught one thing, and then abandoned its old positions to teach something different, and if religious thought was at times found in the ranks of the antagonists of change, it was only as the popular thought was opposed, and as all had been placed in opposition by the earlier forms of scientific teaching. We rightly interpret the facts, only in representing that science both makes its own difficulties and clears them; first presents the imperfect or erroneous views which are to be swept away, and afterwards trains men to more careful sifting of evidence and exercise of thought, thereby clearing and widening its own path.

Thus are we enabled to trace the boundaries of two distinct regions of thought, closely related, yet clearly separated. Science can not do the work of religion, nor can religion do the work of science. Each must fulfil its own part, and abide its proper tests. Science has its own place and its own task. Religion will simply wait upon science, leaving it to make its own discoveries, gladly accepting each one of them as it is established. The most reverend students of the Bible do not regard it as a revelation presenting a key to scientific research; though they do not hesitate to express their conviction that neither in express statement, nor in the spirit inculcated, does it place itself in antagonism to the search for truth; or the claims of any conclusions which can be legitimately described as philosophical or scientific. But its upholders press this consideration specially on scientific men, that the Bible has this title to be regarded as a book for all nations and for all ages, that it has proved itself intelligible to men in ages the least enlightened, and has also maintained a commanding influence in ages specially distinguished and favored by the advance of science and the widening power of literature.

LECTURE III.

INORGANIC ELEMENTS IN THE UNIVERSE.

IN view of the wide range of materials at command, and the limits of the present inquiry, there is need for some definite method of selection, which may secure a careful, though necessarily very general survey of the whole ground. That which seems to give most promise of meeting these requirements is the contemplation in order of the great leading conceptions which have received prominence within recent years in consequence of continued research under strictly scientific methods. These may be said to constitute the scientific revolution of the nineteenth century, giving occasion for reconstructing the popular conceptions of the universe. They claim to mark the truly scientific period, inaugurated by command of instruments never before within reach, allowing an immense advance in the modes of research, and placing the secrets of nature within compass of human observation as they had never been before. The intel lectual conditions for observation and inference no doubt remain simply what they have been; the laws of intelligent inquiry are the same, determining sufficiency of evidence, and trustworthiness in reasoning; but the range of observation has been indefinitely multiplied, and things transcending previous conjecture have become matters of certain observation. The telescope and the microscope provided for this revolution. They brought the universe within range as it had never previously been, and thus making an enormous addition to the sum of human knowledge, suggested new modes of contemplating and explaining the facts which had been familiar through all the ages. There can be no reversal of all this—no return on the old methods. Nor can there be reversal in the sense of overturning presently recognized conclusions. There are indeed hosts of theories of which it may be safely predicted that they will be overturned and forgotten; but a veritable knowledge has been acquired, which will certainly be preserved among the treasures of the race. We now know the constituent elements of many forms of existence, and the laws which determine change and continuance, as these were never previously known; and thus there has been vastly extended for us the range of recognized facts.

To this advance, the whole human race has to adapt itself. It is not merely one class of men, but all; not merely one department of thought, but all departments which must adjust themselves to this new order of things. Religious thought is not thrown into any singular position; it merely shares in the common experience, that is; the common advantage. And we may say religious thought is most prepared for the mighty revolution. This startling success in unlocking the mysteries of nature; this sudden accession to the wealth of our ideas, apt to have an intoxicating effect upon those who value science and nothing higher, awakens reverence and gratitude in the religious thinker. The greater the application of human intelligence to the study of nature, and the greater the discoveries which reward such labor, so much greater becomes the demand upon intelligence in accounting for the origin and continuance of the universe, involving innumerable phases of activity never to be witnessed by ordinary observers who are absorbed in their daily avocations. The supernatural is not more remote from us by such discoveries as science can boast, but is in reality brought nearer. The fancy that enlarged knowledge of the natural, is steadily driving before it all recognition of the supernatural, is one of which thinking men will by and by be ashamed. That men should consider the discovery of the component parts of certain forms of existence, or of the laws of well known movements, as a *final* disposal of the demands of intelligence, only shows how little the intellect of inquirers has been prepared for appreciation of the full demands of reason. In this connection, it should be remembered that the most profoundly scientific, have been the most cautious, least inclined to boast of discovery, or to anticipate the overthrow of the deeper convictions of the moral and spiritual life, which, as the necessaries of life in all ages, are least liable to be touched by any thing belonging to the region of science. Even after every allowance has been made for sanguine and passionate temperament, and for reaction against untenable forms of religious belief among opponents of religion,* the award can not be otherwise than suggested. The facts are already on record bearing on the most testing period,—the transition from an old and restricted knowledge, to a new and greatly enlarged knowledge of the universe,—and the roll of names standing high in the annals of science, while devoted to religious faith and practice, may be accepted as a reasonable forecast of coming results.†

That greater knowledge of nature by discovery of the natural causes in operation, intensifies the rational demand for recognition of Supernatural Intelligence, is the position to be maintained throughout this argument. The most rigid test of this position is to be found in the outstanding scientific conceptions concerning inorganic and organic nature, and the contrasts recognized between lower and higher organisms. The order most suitable for application of this test is progress upwards from the most subordinate forms of

* These allowances may well be made for Professor Clifford, one of the most extravagant assailants of religious faith.

† Professor Tait in answer to Mr. Froude has advanced the evidence. *International Review*, Nov. 1878, vol. v. No. 6. The collected papers have been republished, *Atlas Series*, No. 11.

existence to the most complex organism. A beginning will, therefore, be made with the inorganic world, after which lower organisms may be considered, after that the relative place of higher organisms, and finally the whole class of questions concerning the powers and requirements of mind. In each of these relations, I desire to inquire into the reasonableness of our acknowledgment of the supernatural.

As the world presents a vast range of inorganic existence, we have to consider the most prominent scientific conceptions concerning inorganic elements, as these afford a general view of the material structure of the earth.

Concentrating on this region of observation, and taking no account, meanwhile, of the manifold phases of life, there are two forms of existence to be recognized, Matter and Energy. Matter is solid, visible, tangible; Energy is invisible and intangible, but measurable by the work it is capable of doing. The one may be represented as the solid inert mass, the other as the moving power whose action is the source of continual change. This duality we must regard as essential to the structure of the universe, for it is impossible to identify the two, so as to regard the world as merely a mass of matter. This duality is now commonly admitted as the result of recent scientific investigations. To quote the words of Professor Tait,—"It is only within comparatively recent years that it has been generally recognized that there is something else in the physical universe which possesses to the full as high a claim to objective reality as matter possesses, though it is by no means so tangible, and therefore the conception of it was much longer in forcing itself upon the human mind."* This is Energy. "Just as gold, lead, oxygen, etc., are different kinds of matter, so sound, light, heat, etc., are now ranked as different forms of energy."†

Here, then, is one of the conspicuous results of recent scientific research to which all our thoughts and theories need to adapt themselves. And it must be obvious without argumentation, that theological thought will not experience any serious shock, or

* *Recent Advances in Physical Science*, by P. G. Tait, Professor of Natural Philosophy, University of Edinburgh, p. 17.

† *Ib.* p. 2.

even jolt, in passing over to this new line of rails prepared for it.

Taking these two, Matter and Energy, as distinct, let us concentrate for a little upon each of them separately. Let us first turn attention upon MATTER. This form of existence is most easily contemplated, as most directly presenting itself to observation. A piece of metal may best serve for illustration, such as the *iron* out of which we form so many of our industrial implements. This metal may be mingled through earth or rock; it may be held in solution in water, or made to flow out in liquid form from the furnace; it may be hardened either in the more brittle form of cast iron, or in the more rigid form known as malleable; but through all these changes the material is the same. Further, suppose we were to receive a quantity of ore, and for the sake of experiment were to have part presented in each one of these forms, the quantity would continue exactly the same as was originally received. To quote again from the same author:—"The grand test of the reality of what we call Matter, the proof that it has an objective existence, is its indestructibility and uncreatability—if the term may be used—by any process at the command of man. The value of this test to modern chemistry can scarcely be estimated. In fact we can barely believe that there could have existed an exact science of chemistry had it not been for the early recognition of this property of matter; nor in fact would there be the possibility of a chemical analysis, supposing that we had not the assurance by enormously extended series of previous experiments, that no portion of matter, however small, goes out of existence, or comes into existence in any operation whatever. If the chemist were not certain that at the end of his operations, provided he has taken care to admit nothing and to let nothing escape, the contents of his vessels must be precisely the same in quantity as at the beginning of the experiment, there could be no such thing as chemical analysis."*

If now we press our inquiry further, seeking some explanation of the ultimate nature or structure of matter, that is, the common physical characteristics of matter in all its forms, whether air, water, or solid mass, science has no certain answer to give. There is

* *Recent Advances in Physical Science*, p. 14.

no theory of the ultimate structure of matter which has secured general acceptance. On the contrary, there is the acknowledgment that the complexity of the problem is so great as completely to baffle the present resources of science. There have been discussions, and careful investigations as to the *divisibility of matter*, and it has been generally admitted on rational grounds, that there must be in all matter particles or atoms so minute as to be quite beyond the range of the microscope. This has led to the acceptance of an *atomic theory* as in one form or another applicable to the structure of matter, *belief* in such particles or molecules being a natural result of scientific procedure. I say *belief*, for the existence of such ultimate atoms is not established on experimental evidence, and yet is generally acknowledged; for it is clearly enough recognized that there is a region of faith for science, as for theology, just as there must be for all ordinary exercise of human intelligence. Besides the actual divisibility of matter, we have in the same connection to consider its *compressibility*, for the recognized facts as to compression of iron, for example, or of any metal, seem to imply that there are certain particles related to each other, which can be pressed in upon each other, or brought into nearer proximity. There is, however, a clear limit to compressibility, as there is to divisibility of matter. Even if this be granted, however, we are still without a scientific account of the ultimate structure of matter. This is still a perplexity to be handed on to future workers. There may, indeed, seem to be promise of aid in the analysis of different forms of matter, as in the reduction of water to its constituent gases by the action of a galvanic battery; but such processes, however rich in suggestiveness, are insufficient to advance the main inquiry. It is oftentimes in this very class of experiments, that science at once manifests its power, and discovers the limits which encircle and restrain its efforts. It can decompose, what it can not recompose, thus leaving difficulties as perplexing as before. And besides, even when by analysis the ultimate parts or chemical constituents, of compound substances have been discovered, science is unable to demonstrate that the constituent elements are ultimately composed of distinct atoms, as for example that oxygen and hydrogen are so constituted. We are thus without a science of the ultimate nature of matter. There is, indeed, the suggestion of Sir William Thomson that matter of all kinds may be regarded as of a common nature, only variously compounded, filling space in a fluid state, and that its compressibility can be accounted for on the supposition that its ultimate forms are vortex rings capable of compression and expansion like an india-rubber ball; but this can not be regarded otherwise than as a bold conjecture, beset with a host of difficulties both physical and mathematical which neither Thomson nor any of his fellow-workers in physical science, professes to have yet grappled with.

There are thus before us the chief results of physical science, as to the nature of MATTER, when we specify that it is indestructible, that it consists of ultimate molecules or atoms, and that its compressibility is to be explained by pressure upon such atoms, or cohesion, or comparative closeness of relation between them, this being greater in solids, less in liquids, and least in gases.

From the structure of matter, we are led by science to the consideration of ENERGY, as distinct from matter. These two stand in some respect in contrast with each other. In taking a survey of the physical aspects of the world, we can not limit attention to the mere mass, or to questions bearing on its structure. Observation must now be turned on the perpetual change going on in form, arrangement, and distribution of materials. There is need for a science of all this, in accordance with which the perpetual round of change may be reduced to order by reference to causality and the laws of its operation. Thus we are introduced to our ordinary conceptions concerning *position*, that is, the situation or place of objects, or of masses of material, or even of worlds, to each other; *motion*, or change of position, modifying or altering the relations of objects; and *force*, that is the relative amount or proportion of energy at work for the accomplishment of such changes as those already mentioned. In these connections we are introduced to recently formulated doctrines of *energy*, reached in searching for "the cause which alters or tends to alter a body's natural state of rest," as this problem was indicated in Newton's first law of motion. In the earlier stages of inquiry, attention was directed mainly on the active forces of nature, as these are recognized in operation, admitting of calculation as to rate of movement on the one hand, and relative amount of force on the other. Computations of this kind were necessarily involved in research connected with the movements of the heavenly bodies. When astronomical theory had been matured and a truly scientific understanding of the solar system had been reached, physical science had next to deal with the more general problem raised by the contemplated forces of nature, having a reference at once wider and more minute. It is not possible here to do more than give a very summary view of the doctrine of energy, its mutations, dissipation, and conservation, as developed through study of the laws of gravitation, electricity, light, heat, etc., and now generally accepted. An outline will, however, suffice for an understanding of the general conclusions.

Energy is the term now employed to designate every form of power belonging to the physical world capable of doing work, and of being estimated according to the comparative amount of work it can perform. The whole phenomena of motion thus belong to this department of inquiry. The first distinction here has been described as the difference between *energy of position* and *energy of motion.*[*] Both of these must be taken into account in order to have a full view of the facts. ENERGY OF POSITION, is illustrated by a water-head, or reservoir, where an accumulation of water is laid up in store, ready to be drawn upon for motive power when machinery set up in a position somewhat lower is to be brought into action and made to do the work for which it has been constructed. ENERGY OF MOTION is seen when the storehouse of water is opened and the rush of the current sweeps along the prepared channel descending upon the great wheel, which sets in motion the whole machinery. In such a case as this, the amount of work done by the revolutions of the great wheel is an exact measure of the amount of water which has passed to a lower level. Or let us suppose there is only a limited supply in the water-head, and that there are no feeders, but that the streamlets and springs from which it is supplied, have ceased to flow, and let us suppose that the mill comes to a stand because of failure of motive power, the amount of work done up to that moment is the measure of the energy stored in the water-

* See Appendix III.

head before the sluice was opened. This illustration indicates the mode of calculation to be applied to energy in all its forms, including the great forces of nature, before which human power is as nothing. Taking thus the correlatives position and motion, we may regard the former as preparation for the latter, for, as Professor Balfour Stewart has said, "It is the fate of all kinds of energy of position to be ultimately converted into energy of motion." * On this account, energy of motion most naturally exemplifies what we understand by energy; but on the other hand what has been called the energy of position must be regarded as a power distinctly calculable. If a stone be thrown into the air, the energy expended in propelling it to a certain height, is the exact measure of the energy expended in its descent. There is no need for entering here upon the calculations of the relation between energy and velocity, showing the exact proportion of the one to the other, or the ratio of increase according to velocity, which is expressed in the formula "that the energy varies as the square of the velocity," giving us an exact measure of force.

* *The Conservation of Energy,* by Balfour Stewart, p. 26.

Aided by the conceptions of position and motion, we take the next step when we advance to *transmutation or conversion of energy.* What is made visible to us by motion is the transference of energy from one object or portion of matter to another. And this is the sole explanation of what occurs. There is no such thing known to physical science as the origin or creation of energy; all that is recognized is the disappearance of energy from one position and its appearance in another. If work has been done, energy was somewhere stored capable of doing it; a transmutation has taken place; and the work accomplished is the record of the process. In recognition of this, every machine is merely a more or less skilful contrivance for transmuting energy into a form more convenient or suitable for human purposes. The intelligence of man simply recognizes the law of transmutation, and deals with the problems which arise connected with the mechanical arrangements facilitating the process.

We next advance a further step, only to embrace another phase of the same truth,—the complement of what has been already stated,—that is, the *conservation of energy.*

As we have seen, all that appears in motion, is transmutation or conversion of energy; accordingly it follows, that there is change of position, but no destruction of energy, or absolute disappearance of it from existence. This generalization is illustrated by a most attractive series of observations, introducing to a fuller knowledge of the laws of heat. The natural tendency of ordinary observation is to favor the opinion that when work has been done, energy is spent or lost. And this popular notion, which has a kind of accuracy, in so far as it is needful to make fresh draughts upon available resources, is favored by reference to the economy of our bodily existence constantly renewing its demand for fresh food supply. But this popular tendency is easily explained by the circumstance that ordinary observation makes much more account of the phenomena of motion, than of the development of heat as a direct consequence. The machinist can not, indeed, afford to make little of the consequences of friction; but the ordinary observer makes much more of mass, and complication of mechanical contrivance, and velocity of movement. From this he passes easily to the fabric, or other production, sent forth; and then he may occupy himself with calculations bearing on the expenditure for coals and labor, along with tear and wear of machinery. But scientific observation has concentrated much more on the evolution of heat, and out of this has come the completed theory of the laws of energy. In this way, it became matter of distinct calculation that friction and percussion convert energy into heat.

Along with these observations we have to remark upon an attendant conclusion, which has an important bearing on all speculation concerning the destiny of the universe. I refer to the fact that transmutation of energy involves a deterioration and dissipation of energy. As in the history of energy, improved position adds to the advantage for the doing of work, so transmutation tends to diminish the advantage or utility of the energy for human purposes. Thus the energy expended in working a machine gives return in a product of recognized value, but the energy spent in contending with friction generates heat which is of no practical value in respect of accomplished work. Or as the latter fact has been stated by Professor Balfour Stewart, friction proves "itself to be, not the destroyer of energy, but merely the converter of it into some less apparent, and perhaps less useful form." * In this connection, scientific observation was directed upon the appearance of heat simultaneously with the disappearance of visible energy. Gradually the conception dawned upon scientific observers that *heat is a form of motion*, and this has found general acceptance, although it is impossible to give direct proof of the doctrine. The conclusion has been supported by all the experiments of Davis, Rumford, Joule, Colding, and Helmholtz. This conception having been launched as to the probable explanation of heat, it immediately found, in accordance with the analogies of scientific thought, a greatly extended circle of application. Light and sound came to be classified with heat, as only different forms of motion. It would involve too extended a range to include here a detailed account of these experiments, or to consider what is involved in dissipation of energy, as bearing upon a still wider aspect of the order of things in the universe. I must, therefore, be content with the reference just given to

* *The Conservation of Energy*, p. 36.

the conception of heat as a form of molecular motion; and in doing so may revert to the consideration already adduced, that this is another doctrine of scientific *belief*, of which there is a constant tendency to increase the number, as science widens the range of its inquiries and speculations.

The outstanding general results of science as to the nature of energy are now before us. All observations concerning motion only present to view transmutations of energy, all of them imply that there is no such thing as the origin of energy, and no such thing as its extinction. There is indeed a constant tendency towards the degradation of energy, and a constant equalizing process which may bring to an end the present order of things in the universe. But the leading scientific conception with which we have specially to deal is that expressed in the phrase, "*Conservation of energy,*" which must be regarded as completing our view of inorganic existence along with the other doctrine of the indestructibility of matter. As Professor Tait has expressed it,— "The grand principle of conservation of energy, which asserts that no portion of energy can be put out of existence, and no amount of energy can be brought into existence by any process at our command, is simply a statement of the invariability of the quantity of energy in the universe,—a companion statement to that of the invariability of the quantity of matter." *

The position is now reached at which it becomes possible to combine the results of scientific research as to matter and energy into a harmonious unity, with which to test the view of the world recognized by religious thought. Religion as an intelligent and devotional acknowledgment of a Supreme Being, involves a very clear and definite conception concerning the origin of the universe and its continuance. What is thus implied will be best indicated by negative as well as positive statements, in some such form as the following. First, *negatively*, the world we inhabit does not carry *within it* any explanation of the origin of its own existence; that is to say, neither the materials existing, nor the forces operating, are sufficient to account for its origin; neither can it have had existence without beginning. In *positive* form, the universe can be accounted for only by that which

* *Recent Advances of Physical Science*, p. 17.

transcends itself; the supernatural is the key to the natural; Nature is a creation to be attributed to an Intelligent First Cause.

Are science and religion here in harmony in the form and measure compatible in the circumstances? This qualified and guarded form of the question is obviously required, for religious thought does not profess to be scientific, or in any sense authoritative as to the phenomena of nature, that is, as to the facts which observation alone can ascertain, or as to the immediate causes by which these facts are to be explained. On the other hand, science is exclusively a knowledge of nature, consisting of methodized observations concerning distinct orders of facts, and rational inferences founded upon these. It can not in true sense be concerned with the supernatural, but can only present conclusions as to the order and processes of nature, which by subsequent and independent exercise of our intelligence may be contemplated in their relation to the conception of the supernatural, as Intelligent First Cause. This subsequent exercise of thought, whether critical or constructive, is more properly the task of philosophy, in prosecution of those reflective and speculative exercises, which, proceeding from scientific conclusions as accepted data, consider their intellectual value as contributing towards a theory of the universe. Scientific men will, of course, more or less readily pass over to take some share in such philosophic speculation; just as religious men, purely under the impulse of religious interests, will be more or less disposed to do, in proportion to the range of their intellectual life. What is here said is not intended as an argument for any restriction upon such speculation on the part either of scientific or of religious men, for such questions are common property, and the arguments bearing upon them are to be tested by all. But it is of some consequence, specially in the present unsettled and sensitive state of the public mind, that it be clearly recognized that science is not itself responsible for the thoughts of scientific men on these questions; and that religion is not responsible for the thoughts of religious men upon them. Science can not determine any thing as to a philosophy of the supernatural, any more than religion can determine any thing as to a science of nature. Whether we take the violent and even passionate antipathy to any acknowledgment of the supernatural which is found in the Essays of Clifford, or the profoundly reverential acknowledgment of the Deity in the writings and life of Faraday, science is to be credited with neither. And so in like manner, when we have violent denunciations of science professedly in the name of religion, or intelligent appreciation of its high value from accredited upholders of religious truth, religion itself is to be credited with neither the one nor the other. This is a matter which comes within the range of ordinary intelligence. It may indeed belong to philosophy to formulate and develop the arguments in strict harmony with the recognized laws of mind; but it belongs equally to all men to estimate the general sweep and range of acquired knowledge as to the structure and order of the universe, as bearing upon the more general conceptions to be rationally entertained regarding its government. With this branch of the subject, ordinary thought may readily deal without entanglement in technicalities.

There is as we have seen a *duality* of existence in the inorganic structure of the world, and a continual succession of changes, on account of the interaction of these two. Different forms of matter stand in different relations; and these relations are being constantly interchanged by the transmutation of energy. Thus taking the world as presented to us, it has a constitution which requires for its explanation that we go beyond every thing to be found within itself. The matter in the universe can not account for the energy; nor can the energy account for the matter; and the relations between the two must find explanation in something higher than both. What their source may be, science is incapable of telling; it can not contribute towards satisfying the requirements of the law of causality in view of the mutual relations of matter and energy which it has itself revealed. But equally by what it has revealed, and by acknowledgment of its inability to transcend the limits of its own discoveries, does it present harmony with religious thought in the form and measure in which it is possible that such harmony could be manifested. Discovering the objective existence of matter and energy, and the laws in accordance with which the latter acts upon the former, it presents an unsolved problem affording the most direct and positive testimony possible to science in support of the existence of a First Cause, transcending the universe itself. How matter and energy came into being, it can not tell; but it most explicitly declares that by no power existing and operating within range of observation is it possible either to add to the sum of existence, or in the least degree to diminish it. Religious thought could expect nothing more direct and explicit in the form of scientific testimony as confirmation of its fundamental position. Scientific thought while dealing with inorganic existence could not, even by a single line of approach, be brought nearer to the actual support of religious belief.

Here the question may be raised,—May not the world have existed from eternity? In the answer to this question there are several considerations requiring to be distinguished. First, science has no testimony to offer, inasmuch as it does not get beyond the area of laws now operating. Second, the testimony of science concerning the world as now existing is inconsistent with the supposition of its eternal existence. The matter which is constantly operated upon by energy distinct from itself, does not possess the property of self-subsistence; neither does the energy which is constantly undergoing change. Continual transition or change from one phase of existence, or set of relations, to another, is a mark of the not-abiding, an evidence of subjection to, and dependence on, what is beyond and above itself. The non-enduring, or ever-changing, is constantly pointing to the ever-enduring.

Full understanding of the situation of things as discovered by science will produce a much deeper impression on the public mind than has yet been effected. The reasonableness of this expectation will readily appear, if only some few of the positions be placed conspicuously in view.

It is of special consequence to note that science has in this direction *finished its work*, and reached its *ultimatum*, in demonstrating the physical impossibility of either increasing or diminishing the existing sum total of matter, or of energy. The conclusions are not such as can be regarded as provisional, liable to be overreached, modified, or enlarged, by what may afterwards be discovered. We are so much influenced at present,—and scientific men share in the experience, as well as others,—by the general and well-grounded expectation of the unceasing advance of science, that it is peculiarly easy in sight of a great general problem such as the origin and government of the world, to overlook the significance of ultimate conclusions in given directions. In this way, we too readily fall into the delusive tendency of regarding accredited conclusions as still hanging in a measure of uncertainty, or at least as having a dubious future before them, because they border upon the region of the unknown so far as science is concerned, or upon a realm of mystery, which science regards either with aversion, or with cherished determination of attack. In the present singularly favorable position of science, it is impossible for the public mind to escape this tendency; but it becomes only the more imperative to distinguish as occasion offers, those conclusions which are to be taken as final. This is of immense consequence as bearing upon general conceptions concerning the universe.

That matter can not be originated, and can not by even a single atom be destroyed, is one of those ultimate statements, upon which physical science itself relies as on a foundation. This is a universally accredited truth, that "no portion of matter, however small, goes out of existence or comes into existence in any operation whatever." * The wonderful chemical laboratory of living organism may change many forms of matter into living tissue, but all returns again to its place in the inorganic mass. Material may pass from one phase into another, but there is nothing more than change. The sum total of material existence is unaltered. To suggest the contrary,—and specially to do so in the name of science,—were to bring science face to face with the conceptions rejected as alien to its very nature; for to say that matter may be originated, is to affirm *creation*; to say that it may be destroyed, is to affirm the possibility of *annihilation*; and these two are beyond the range of science, and if once admitted within its boundaries, they would destroy science itself.

So it is when we pass over to the doctrine of energy. The same clear and ultimate conclusion is proclaimed. The doctrine of the conservation of energy is the *ultimatum* on

* Tait's *Recent Advances*, p. 15.

which physical science finds sure and firm foothold. In those two ultimate positions of scientific research concerning inorganic existence, religion finds support, and that of a kind so powerful, that science itself depends upon its immovability.

There is, however, a further point connected with the doctrine of energy, which deserves consideration as bearing on the tendency to anticipate an indefinite line of progression in the history of this world, that is, deterioration or degradation in the form of energy, while it continues of equal amount. The efficient value of energy is according to the possibilities of transformation or transmutation. But its use implies limitation of the available forms, or steady deterioration of value. "Thus the energy of the universe is, on the whole, constantly passing from higher to lower forms, and therefore the possibility of transformation is becoming smaller and smaller, so that after the lapse of sufficient time all higher forms of energy must have passed from the physical universe, and we can imagine nothing as remaining, except those lower forms which are incapable, so far as we yet know, of any further transformation."* Such a statement of the position, though it can not be regarded as an ultimate one in scientific research, is so obviously a deduction from present knowledge that it must to some extent modify prevailing conceptions. It may, indeed be suggested that some catastrophe may terminate the present order of things, and that some action of the law of gravitation may combine the fragments of worlds, and give a fresh start with new combinations of energy; but the bare suggestion of this implies a much wider range for scientific research than any thing yet known to us, and at the same time a larger demand upon intelligence in the control and regulation of what must nevertheless seem to us violent catastrophes. Such speculation, if it may warrantably find encouragement under purely scientific conditions, religious thought will neither gainsay nor resist; but will find itself in no perplexity to accept.

Waiving, however, all speculation as to the possible future of the physical universe, we here concentrate attention on the past; we take the most recent scientific testimony as to the structure of the physical universe, as

* *Recent Advances*, p. 20.

it bears on the problem concerning the origin of our world. Here the testimony of science is clearly and unmistakably in favor of the creation or absolute origin of matter and energy, in the only form in which science can bear any testimony on the subject. It is, of course, impossible that science should present direct testimony to the fact of creation, as it is impossible that history should; for such a fact as creation must be entirely beyond the range of science. But in testifying to the indestructibility and uncreatability of matter under the conditions capable of being investigated by observational science; and in bearing the same testimony as to the energy in the world, it offers all the support it is capable of offering to the reality of the supernatural,—testifying to the dependence of nature on some power altogether transcending itself. But here I prefer rather to use the words of a purely scientific observer. When dealing with the doctrine of energy, and specially with the consequences of dissipation of energy, Professor Tait uses these words,—"As it alone is able to lead us, by sure steps of deductive reasoning, to the necessary future of the universe—necessary, that is, if physical laws remain forever unchanged—so it enables us distinctly to say that the present order of things has *not* been evolved through infinite past time by the agency of laws now at work; but must have had a distinctive beginning, a state beyond which we are totally unable to penetrate; a state, in fact, which must have been produced by other than the now visibly acting causes."* This is the utmost that science can say, bearing on the great problem of the origin of the universe; and nothing more powerful could be said in direct testimony to the reality of the supernatural, and the reasonableness of Christian faith, thus shown to be in complete harmony with science.

It is not here suggested that all scientific men would employ such language as that now quoted, or even readily acquiesce in its use. I have been careful to indicate, that a passionately excited antagonism to any recognition of the supernatural is avowed by some scientific men. Accordingly, it must be granted that the conclusion here stated is not so manifest a deduction as to preclude denial. The testimony of the senses commonly terminates dispute, but such testimony is not available as

* *Recent Advances*, p. 22.

to the reality of the supernatural. The only testimony that can be given here must be of a different kind; and if there be some who refuse to credit anything save what comes within range of the senses, or is deducible directly and simply from what the senses make known, there is no help for them. Neither science, nor philosophy, nor religion can deliver them from the narrow round of materialism. But neither science, nor philosophy, nor religion, can restrict itself to the testimony of the senses. A deeper, and wider range of inquiry is demanded of the man who would walk at large in the vast field spread out in nature. All human life is subjected to the test of accepting evidence other than that the senses supply. If some refuse to submit to this deeper and wider test, narrowing their convictions accordingly, others are not to be restricted in this way, nor are they to be influenced by such determination even on the part of highly distinguished scientific men. For, it can not be overlooked that this is not a question of science, nor does it imply any thing but an ordinary exercise of intelligence. The one test for the public mind is this,—Is it or is it not true that not an atom of matter can be originated or destroyed? Is the doctrine of the conservation of energy to be taken as scientifically demonstrated? These things science must decide, and beyond these, all is clear for ordinary intelligence. Of the testimony of science on these two questions there is no doubt whatever. Religion, therefore, has no conflict with science here; it simply accepts the teaching of science, finding in it ample support for its fundamental position. What creation really means, or how we can fittingly represent it to our minds, does not in the least affect the question here under discussion, for these are not points on which science can offer any testimony. Nor have the defenders of religion any complaint to urge against the claims which science makes to explain all that belongs to nature. But when those who make the largest claims for science, acknowledge that science is baffled here, their testimony gains in value by reason of the strength of their antipathy to the acknowledgment of the miraculous. When from an accredited scientific witness we have these words:—"The investigation of nature does not shrink from enrolling life and the processes of life in the world of the comprehensible," followed up by this explicit statement, "We are foiled only at the conception of matter and force";* the claims of science are raised to the highest pitch; and yet its insuperable limits are clearly defined. The defender of the harmony of scientific with religious thought has nothing more to desire. The very place where science comes to a halt, acknowledging that its utmost boundary has been reached, is the place where it is demonstrated that scientific thought and religious are not involved in real conflict.

* *The Doctrine of Descent*, by Oscar Schmidt, p. 20.

LECTURE IV.

ORGANIZED EXISTENCE: LIFE AND ITS DEVELOPMENT.—(DARWIN'S "THEORY OF EVOLUTION.")

IN prosecuting our inquiry as to the most recent advances in science, we pass now from inorganic to organic existence; from the testimony of physicists, to that of zoölogists. This transition in itself starts a scientific problem, beyond which we are carried onward to a distinct and very complicated area of existence, higher in order, and pressing upon attention an incalculable variety of details, exceedingly difficult to harmonize. In the earlier stage of physical research, all observation and experiment lead forward to general results, which gain ready acceptance because they may be said to be involved in scientific procedure itself. In this more advanced stage it is otherwise. In the former, unorganized matter is the same everywhere; and the laws of energy can be studied with equal facility in Europe or in America, in northern latitudes or in southern. But when we begin to direct attention upon life in its manifold forms, as these are scattered all over the world, multitudes of distinct observations have to be prosecuted, and their results slowly accumulated, before even the most competent workers can occupy a position from which it is possible to make a beginning with our forecast of general conclusions. Even in the most favorable circumstances, a great deal must be left to problematic inference, and even to imagination. Gatherings of facts may be recorded in a manner which places them beyond reach of doubt, while theories founded upon them hang long in suspense, waiting confirmation on condition of being able to endure protracted criticism, and manifold applications. This accounts for the difficulty experienced in finding ready to hand general conclusions which have secured universal acceptance, when we begin to move somewhat freely over the wide regions presenting the manifold problems of organized existence. And as it is solely with general conclusions, that religious thought is concerned, some share of perplexity must attach to the attempt to discuss the question of harmony. We must here therefore be considerably involved in questions affecting theories which have gained wide favor in scientific circles, as well as with clearly recorded and certain results. Some general questions, such as that affecting the classification of animals, must be regarded as peculiarly scientific. Whether the classification of Linnæus, or of Cuvier, or some other more recently suggested, is to be preferred, is a matter which does not here concern us. But a theory of the origin of species must be considered, because it is not purely scientific, but brings science into direct relation with common thought as to the order of the universe, and may therefore stand related to religious thought.

Immediately on directing attention to organized existence,—to LIFE in any form,—we encounter a new problem, namely the relation of the organized to the unorganized. How is the appearance of this higher order of existence to be accounted for? Can we find in the nature of matter, and in the mechanical and chemical laws influencing its position and combination, any explanation of the appearance of life in the world? Or must we regard life as a new and higher fact, unexplained by reference to the lower form of existence, and incapable of explanation in this way? Whether there is a clear line of demarcation between vegetable and animal life is a comparatively subordinate question. It is the wider and more perplexing question which most fundamentally affects our general conceptions as to the history and government of the world? And when this question is pressed singly,—how can we account for the appearance of life in the world?—science has no answer to present. Life still remains a mystery in scientific times, as it had been in past ages. Much has been written as to the origin of species; nothing to any purpose has yet been said as to the origin of life itself. The secrets of the universe in this respect have eluded discovery, and a constrained silence is the consequence.

But if science itself has nothing to say as to this fundamental problem, scientific men have much to say as to the probability of a true solution of the mystery being forthcoming. There is in many quarters an expectation that we may yet understand the physical principles, that is, the mechanical and chemical combinations, which go to explain life as a working organism.* The suggestions of Rumford and Joule may yet bear results in this direction, for it is matter of general agreement that living organism may be regarded as an engine doing a given amount of work, on condition of being supplied with a given amount of fuel in the form of nourishment. When therefore Rumford suggests that the animal is a more economical engine than any of the mechanical contrivances which man constructs, and when Joule advances considerably beyond this to suggest that the animal more resembles an electro-magnetic engine, than a heat engine, it seems quite within the range of possibility that in some such direction discovery may yet be made of the physical principles involved in life.

This, however, leaves untouched the deeper question as to the *origin of life.* We are entirely ignorant of any beginning of life which is not traced directly to a preceding living organism. Either, as in the case of plants, there is increase of life by fission, or separation from an earlier growth, or by means of seed grown upon the parent plant; or, as in the case of animals, by germ or ovum. But the

* Tait's *Recent Advances*, p. 23.

question of the origin of life is remote from us historically, and perplexing to us experimentally. If we seek guidance historically, we turn to geology, and learn that the structure of the earth has involved successive formations. The materials of the earth's crust are not thrown together confusedly, but "exhibit a certain order of arrangement";* the mineral masses are partly aqueous, partly igneous, in formation; according as they are one or other, they contain organic remains, or are marked by their absence. All that can be inferred from the data thus afforded is that at a certain period in the world's history, when temperature and other conditions affecting the possibility of organic existence were favorable, life appeared. As to the cause of its appearance, geology can give no testimony. If next, we refer to palæontology, we learn of the existence of colossal animals which have long since become extinct; but such researches only widen our acquaintance with different orders of animals, contributing nothing towards the solution of the problem concerning the origin of life. The experimental science of the present day, with

* Lyell's *Elements of Geology*, p. 2.

all the advantages arising from microscopical observation, is altogether unable to offer any explanation. Experiments for the purpose of testing the probability of "spontaneous generation" have been already described, and their failure leaves experimental science without any direct testimony; while their history yields powerful indirect evidence in support of the position that origin of life apart from germ is unknown.

It is, however, desirable here, in order to give completeness to our view of the present situation, to remark that among scientific men there are some who have no expectation of a scientific explanation of the origin of life; while others are exceedingly hopeful that such explanation may be reached, in the latter class appearing naturally all those who openly proclaim against what they name an "incomprehensible act of creation," and voluntarily place themselves in antagonism to religious thought. It is, therefore, of some consequence to indicate the grounds on which such opposite views rest. On the one side, Professor Tait, while suggesting the possibility of yet discovering the physical principles which determine life, nevertheless adds, "Let no one imagine that, should we ever penetrate this mystery, we shall thereby be enabled to produce, except from life, even the lowest form of life." * On the other hand Professor Schmidt of Strasburg maintains the opposite view, affirming that "the investigation of nature does not shrink from enrolling *life*, and the processes of life in the world of the comprehensible." † This latter assertion is not to be accounted for on the ground that Schmidt is the ardent admirer and defender of the theory of origin of species by natural selection, for it is clear, as he maintains in replying to Max Müller, that "the origin of life has in fact nothing to do with actual Darwinism, or natural selection, unless the principle of selection be extended to the inorganic world of matter." ‡ Mr. Darwin himself does not suggest any such extension, and his theory of species is not chargeable with it. It should, indeed, be clearly recognized on all hands that the naturalist confines himself to a narrower range of inquiry, taking existing phases of life as the subject of his study. Accordingly, whoever claims that the origin of life comes within

* *Recent Advances*, p. 24. † *Doctrine of Descent*, p. 20.

‡ *Ib.* p. 161.

the compass of science, does so on the ground that there is no demarcation between the organic and the inorganic,—that the former may arise directly from the latter,—and so he commits himself to a doctrine of descent worldwide in its application, involving development in the world of all its varied phases of existence from a mass of unorganized matter.

This explains the difference of opinion among scientific men as to the possibility of accounting for the origin of life. A certain number deny the possibility, as they do the possibility of explaining scientifically the origin of matter on the explicit ground indicated by Laplace,—"Present events are connected with the events of the past by a link resting on the obvious principle, that a thing can not begin to exist without a cause which produces it."* They do not find in inorganic matter sufficient cause to account for life, and their expectations are restricted accordingly. Those who cherish a contrary expectation, do not vindicate it by contradiction of the obvious principle enunciated by Laplace, or even by maintaining that inorganic matter is adequate to produce living organism. They cling

* *Introduction to the Theory of Science*, p.

to the more general and doubtful position that no limits are to be assigned to science, or as it is often stated, all nature belongs to the comprehensible. The failure of past experiments is no proof that inevitable failure awaits other experiments which may yet be made. To abandon expectation seems to them to be unfaithful to science. In this fashion, Professor Schmidt declares that "to any one who holds open the possibility that, even now, animate may be evolved from inanimate, without the mediation of progenitors, *the first origin of life in this natural method is at once self-evident.*" * To this view the other side may legitimately reply, that if the origin of life be as easily accounted for, as provision is here made for the "self-evident," science will soon be at a discount. To those regarding the matter from without, and waiting for testimony as to what is scientifically established, it is clear that there is no explanation of the origin of life; and I think it will be most commonly held that the weight of reason as to expectations for the future lies with those who abandon the anticipation of any scientific explanation. There is, however, in actual conclusions on

* *Doctrine of Descent*, p. 163.

scientific evidence nothing involving conflict with religious conviction; and allowance will be made for continued and extended experiments, provided only that the "holding open the possibility," does not make the probability "self-evident."

Passing thus from the unsolved problem of the origin of life,—with the attendant acknowledgment that there is no scientific theory of the world's descent from primordial atoms, we advance to the testimony of science concerning different orders of life, and their relations to each other. Here there is no restriction as to the use of scientific methods; there is wide range for free action by the hosts of observers required for the work. A sense of the relief which this implies, in contrast with the hampering restraints surrounding the earlier question, imparts to the words of Schmidt a more jubilant tone, as he says, "Between beginning and end, we naturalists may do as we please." *

In this region it will be universally admitted that the development of species by selection is the conception which has gained greatest hold upon the scientific mind within

* *Doctrine of Descent*, p. 162.

recent times. Accordingly it seems better to begin with an outline of this theory, and of its history as developed by Mr. Darwin, keeping, however, steadily in view the range of problem with which the theory has to deal.

As already remarked the origin of life is a problem quite distinct, and the theory of selection does not entangle itself by maintaining origin of life by development from unorganized matter. Mr. Darwin clearly guarded himself against responsibility for such a conception of its origin.* Restricting thus far, we have to keep in view the vast range of the problem demanding scientific explanation.

Animal life manifests itself by spontaneous movement,—movement from within the living organism, in contrast with movement caused by energy applied from without. This holds true of every living germ, from which a mature animal form may be developed. This is the test of the presence of life under the microscope in minute germinal structures otherwise incapable of observation. In its lowest known form life appears in a minute vessel containing so much nourishment, which is within a nucleus or vital centre from which move-

* *Origin of Species*, p. 577.

ment originates.* This depends for its development on external conditions such as heat and moisture.† Advance in the scale is connected with greater complexity in the organism. As we ascend, separate organs appear, fulfilling distinct functions, and controlled by means of a nerve system whose ramifications are according to the intricacy of the organism. The appearance of such a nerve system implies sensibility and motor activity, provision for an *experience* more or less varied, and *movement* in some measure according with it, or adapted to it. From a nerve system consisting of a centre and a few fibres, we gradually ascend, until in the higher vertebrate orders, we find a vast system of nerves harmonized and governed from a grand centre or terminus constituting the brain.‡ With the steadily advancing complexity of nerve system, there is great diversity in the orders of animals, in the variety of actions of which they are capable, in adaptation to different conditions of life, and in the modes in which they obtain subsistence. The scientific problem is—How far can we account for all this complex system of things by the action of natural causes?

As we are here specially concerned with

* See Appendix VII. † See Appendix V. ‡ See Appendix IV.

ruling conceptions, and only indirectly with details, the relations of the animal and vegetable kingdoms may be passed, with the acknowledgment that the two are obviously distinct, and yet that the vegetable very nearly merges into the animal at certain points, as illustrated by sensibility, if not by locomotion. So may we waive discussion of the classification of animals, which involves important points closely connected with the main question. Allowing that the wonderful diversity in animal organization, may admit of different modes of classification; and yet granting that the structure of the animal economy in all its forms proceeds on common principles, which must lead to practical agreement as to modes of classification; we deal with the single question as to the natural causes serving to explain different orders.

Mr. Darwin's suggestion, largely supported by evidence from many quarters, and now commanding a very general support is, that all this diversity may be regarded as the product of a long process of development. This theory takes the whole orders of existence into one sweep. The lowest type of animal life presents to view the beginning of a protracted history; the highest order of animate existence indicates the stage of advance at which we observe things at the present period. For such a theory the history of individual development belonging to whatever order, and the history of distinct orders as indicating improvement and deviation of whatever aspect, present evidence of special value. The most important causes relied upon as contributing to the formation of a scientific theory may be presented under these four heads—(1) The action of external causes as provided for by environment; (2) power of adaptability within each organism, providing for changes according to requirement from without, which may be described as "adaptive changes of structure;" (3) "the struggle for existence," in accordance with which the strongest gain the mastery and consequent advantage in obtaining the means of subsistence; and (4) "natural selection" among the sexes, giving to the offspring all advantages according to the laws of hereditary descent.

The essential feature in this theory is the *power of adaptability inherent in the organism.*

This is postulated as characteristic of all organized existence; and it is implied, that this power of adaptability multiplies in a degree approximating to the measure of complexity belonging to the organism. The inherent capacity for deviation is thus much less in the mollusk than in the bird; and in the bird much less than in the quadruped. Thus the development process which must, according to this view, have been exceedingly slow in the earlier stages, must have been greatly accelerated when more complex organisms had come into existence, and all the advantages accrued from greater diver sity of materials. Such is a brief outline of the theory; and looked at simply as a theory, there is a manifest attraction in the boldness of the conception, and the wide sweep of the generalization which it includes. Taken merely as an intellectual representation setting forth a conceivable order of things in the universe, it has a great deal to command attention and awaken interest. It is, indeed, a novelty in the history of scientific thought, and as such at variance with previous conceptions, both scientific and non-scientific. But it is no more at variance with religious thought, than with ordinary notions of preceding times; while to the author whose name is now associated with it all over the scientific world, it is a more striking testimony of the marvels of creative power,* than notions previously current, which regarded it as historically true that every existing variety of animal was launched into being by a distinct creative act. Whatever may be the ultimate view of the history of life on the earth, based on purely scientific data,—and we are still a far way removed from what may be regarded as scientific evidence for such a view,—the fewer the primordial forms to which the multiplicity of existing species can be traced, the greater is the marvel which science presents, and the more convincing becomes the intellectual necessity by which we travel back to a Supernatural Intelligence as the source of all. On the other hand, the slow process by which scientific research tends to make out the natural history of living organisms far removed from each other in the scale of being, tracing many groups to a common parentage, and assigning their appearance in the world to

* *Origin of Species*, p. 577.

distinct periods in its history, will be seen to be so far anticipated and favored by the graphic description of the introduction of animal life given in the opening page of revelation, where different orders are assigned to successive epochs.

While, however, these things are said at the outset, as affording commencement for the study of an evolution theory, and de livering us from the supposition that there is an inevitable antagonism between science and recognition of the supernatural, we revert to the ruling principle for this whole inquiry, that science must prosecute its own researches, unfettered by forecast of consequences; and that the Bible is not to be handled as if it were a book of science, for it neither lays restraints upon human inquiry, nor delivers us from the need for it.

The best method for entering upon a study of the theory of evolution by natural selection is to take Mr. Darwin's own account of the manner in which it began to take shape before his mind. In his "historical sketch of the recent progress of opinion on the origin of species," * he traces to Lamark the first sug-

* *The Origin of Species*, xiii. 4th ed.

gestions on the subject, directing public attention to the question in 1801; thereafter a succession of naturalists including St. Hilaire, Wells, and Patrick Matthew, from separate and incidental observations, dwelt upon the difficulty of distinguishing species, and on the evidence of an archetypal idea, or common plan of structure, being applicable in the history of whole orders. Mr. Darwin then gives the following biographical references at the outset,—"When on board H. M. S. 'Beagle,' as naturalist, I was much struck with certain facts in the distribution of the organic beings inhabiting South America, and in the geological relations of the present to the past inhabitants of that continent. These facts seemed to throw some light on the origin of species—that mystery of mysteries, as it has been called by one of our greatest philosophers. On my return home, it occurred to me in 1837, that something might perhaps be made out on this question by patiently accumulating and reflecting on all sorts of facts which could possibly have any bearing on it. After five years' work I allowed myself to speculate on the subject, and drew up some short notes; these I enlarged in 1844 into a sketch of the conclusions which then seemed to me probable: from that period to the present day I have steadily pursued the same object." * Such is Mr. Darwin's opening paragraph in the now celebrated *Origin of Species.* No one interested in such investigations will hesitate to approve and trust the "patiently accumulating and reflecting on all sorts of facts;" nor can there be any hesitation in granting the warrantableness of his beginning to speculate as to the probable results. On the other hand, even the most ardent admirers of the evolution theory can not refuse to allow that only its principles are certain, while its ultimate form is still matter of conjecture and speculation. Quite divergent lines of speculation have found a start within the compass of the phenomena brought under review, and it is already apparent that opposite tendencies of thought have effected a lodgment under the common name of evolution. In these circumstances there is no direct call, as there are no proper materials, for attempting a reconciliation between the principles of religion, and definite scientific conclusions as to the origin of species. We are

* *The Origin of Species*, p. 1.

still occupying that position which makes historical treatment of the subject the most appropriate, leaving to speculation the probable lines of adjustment which may render possible a wider induction bearing on a general theory of the universe.

The observations of Alfred Russell Wallace in the Malay Archipelago led towards the same conclusions as those indicated by Darwin, to whom Mr. Wallace dedicated his book,* giving the results of research extending from 1854 to 1862, and in confirmation of Darwin's theory, though differing on important points, Wallace published in 1870 his *Contribution to the Theory of Natural Selection.* Mr. Darwin's views when first promulgated received decided though somewhat guarded support from Sir Charles Lyell, whose geological studies marked him out as a highly qualified witness on the subject, and were strongly favored by Dr. Hooker, author of *Introduction to the Australian Flora,* while they encountered not a little criticism, and were met with announcements of formal reservations, on the part of distinguished naturalists.

* *Malay Archipelago,* 1869.

A fuller statement as to the history of his own thought was given by Mr. Darwin in the fifth edition of his work, and also in a letter to Hæckel, author of the bolder venture as to the *History of the Creation*, and the *Evolution of Man*. This letter to Hæckel may be given here as having considerable value in its bearing on the formation of the theory of evolution. After referring to his early researches as to lower forms of life, Mr. Darwin proceeds thus—"Having reflected much on the foregoing facts, it seemed to me probable that *allied species* were descended from a common ancestor. But during several years I could not conceive how each form could have been modified so as to become admirably adapted to its place in nature. I began therefore to study domesticated animals and cultivated plants, and after a time perceived that *man's power of selecting and breeding* from certain individuals was the most powerful of all means in the production of *new races*. Having attended to the habits of animals and their relations to the surrounding conditions, I was able to realize the severe *struggle for existence* to which all organisms are subjected; and my geological observations had allowed me to appreciate to a certain extent the duration of past geological periods. With my mind thus prepared, I fortunately happened to read Malthus's *Essay on Population*; and the idea of natural selection through the struggle for existence at once occurred to me. Of all the subordinate points in the theory, the last which I understood was the cause of the *tendency* in the descendants from a common progenitor *to diverge* in character." * This short passage in personal history may considerably aid others in their study of the theory.

This letter may with advantage be supplemented by one or two brief extracts from *The Origin of Species.* In one of his most recent editions, our author says,—"It may be metaphorically said, that natural selection is daily and hourly scrutinizing throughout the world the slightest variations, rejecting those that are bad, preserving and adding up all that are good; silently and insensibly working, whenever and wherever opportunity offers, at the improvement of each organic being in relation to its organic and inorganic condi-

* The passage is quoted as given by Schmidt in his *Doctrine of Descent*, p. 132. Italics are inserted to guide the eye of the reader to the successive stages.

tions of life." Such a metaphorical representation attributing to nature different processes, such as scrutinizing, rejecting, preserving, and working, considerably aids us by pointing to the *intellectual* conditions involved in the acceptance of the theory of evolution. To this it may suffice if there be added the closing passage in our author's work on species, indicating his view of the relation of all to the supernatural. It is in these words—"Thus, from the war of nature, from famine and death, the most exalted object which we are capable of conceiving,* namely, the production of the higher animals, directly follows. There is grandeur in this view of life, with its several powers, having been originally breathed by the Creator into a few forms or into one; and that whilst this planet has gone cycling on according to the fixed law of gravity, from so simple a beginning endless forms most beautiful and most wonderful have been, and are being evolved." † On this passage, Schmidt has remarked—"In this concession, Darwin has certainly been untrue to himself; and it satisfies neither those who believe in the con-

* Referring to organized being.

† *Origin of Species*, p. 577.

tinuous work of creation by a personal God, nor the partisans of natural evolution." In this criticism we have a good example of the manner in which an impression of conflict is fostered. The rejoinder to Schmidt is obvious. Those who value religion seek no concessions, but desire to banish from scientific and philosophic writing all thought tending in this direction. If, however, needless complications are to be avoided, we must have exact statements of the relative positions. The sentence just quoted involves a misrepresentation equally of religion and science. Belief in the supernatural does not imply belief in *a continuous work of creation*, and therefore does not carry any thing inherently antagonistic to the conception of evolution under natural law. On the other hand, belief in evolution of species under the action of natural law does not decide the question, concerning *the origin of life*, just as a science of nature can decide nothing concerning the supernatural.

Professor Schmidt is, however, so far from clearly and consistently recognizing the exact limit of the theory, that within the compass of a single page he first affirms the limitation, and then denies it. First vindicating Darwin from the attack of Max Müller as to beginning and end of living organism, he says, "The origin of life has in fact nothing to do with actual Darwinism, or natural selection, unless the principle of selection be extended to the inorganic world of matter,"* an entanglement which Schmidt is willing to avoid, and which Darwin carefully shuns, distinctly stating that "Science in her present state does not countenance the belief that living creatures are now ever produced from inorganic matter."† But Schmidt has no sooner placed himself behind this line of defence, than he attacks Darwin for acknowledging origin of life by creation, maintaining that "it is directly incompatible with the doctrine of descent."‡ The theorist must take either one side or the other. Either he must maintain that the theory of descent has "nothing to do with the origin of life," and in that case there is no conflict with religious thought; or that the theory of descent is incompatible with creation, and in that case there is conflict with religious thought, and at the same

* *Doct. of Descent*, p. 161–2.

† *Origin of Species*, 4th ed. p. 143.

‡ *Doct. of Descent*, 162.

time inconsistency with science, in respect of its own definition as an explanation of nature, and in respect of its own results which do not involve "spontaneous generation," but do include the position that not a single particle of matter can be originated or destroyed by any power recognized in operation. No one will "dispute the claims of the investigation of nature to its logical inferences," but "where the material substratum is deficient," most reasonable men will demand that distinct acknowledgment be made of the fact, and that the boundaries of science be defined accordingly. If, however, any one be inclined to maintain that "where the material substratum is deficient," all inquiry must terminate, and human thought must refuse to go further, or to attempt to rise higher, this certainly is not science, but an illogical attempt to make the science of nature commensurate with the boundaries of thought,—an arbitary declaration that "the causal series" within the material universe is the sum total of causality. Such an affirmation can not warrantably attach itself to a theory of descent, as it can not be tested by observational methods, but altogether by reference to the laws of thought determining the value of rationalizing processes. The theory of "natural evolution," implies evolution from something; it postulates a beginning from which it takes procedure, and it exhausts itself in observations concerning such deviations as occur in the annals of natural history. If, therefore, any of "the partisans of natural evolution," take up a position involving denial of a rational acknowledgment of the supernatural, they isolate themselves in so doing, leaving the theory free from responsibility as to their attitude, and taking upon themselves the logical necessity for vindicating their position on grounds with which the theory of evolution itself has no concern.

Having thus vindicated the theory of natural evolution from all share in the denial of creation, and having entered a protest upon purely scientific grounds against the attempt to translate a scientific theory concerning a limited order of facts within the universe into a metaphysical theory concerning the origin of the universe, we are in a position to concentrate upon the theory itself as an attempt to provide a scientific explanation of the history of living organism. And this is here done with the view of ascertaining, in a general and necessarily restricted manner, the value of the evidence presented for its acceptance, thereby ascertaining its relations to the essential characteristics of religious thought.

The first and simplest part of the task is to indicate the favorable impression it has made on the minds of men,—the conquest it has already won for itself,—as a theory carrying within it a large amount of truth, whatever may be its final form, after the very intricate and difficult questions involved have been carefully examined. The theory has carried general approval for the position that "allied species are descended from a common ancestor," or, stating the same view in the manner suggested by experiment, that it is possible to obtain in the history of a single race of animals, considerable deviations in structure, and to give these deviations fixedness or permanence by continuance of selected features along the line of hereditary descent. This has been amply illustrated by the examples of the various orders of pigeons, and of dogs· both classes of animals having been largely experimented upon, and the distinct varieties being easily recognized and popularly known

Comparatively little hesitation exists as to acknowledging that the different orders of pigeons have had a common ancestry; and that the same may be said of the different races of dogs. These examples afford the governing conception of the evolution theory, presenting the type of evidence which has led on to the wider generalization. Under the discussions which the theory has originated facts previously familiar have been contemplated in a different light, as bearing upon a general plan or order of procedure apparent in the history of organized existence. The consequent gain for the theory is altogether favorable to the restricted doctrine that allied species have had a common descent, or that a single type of organism may under the law of evolution lead to the appearance of different orders or races of animals.

The clear advance thus made in our conceptions of the history of the universe will appear by simple statement of negative results following from the admission of the modified form of doctrine just given. These involve the rejection of views previously held, not by religious men in religious interests, but by men generally, as the natural consequence of the want of scientific investigations fitted to guide the public mind. So far as a general conclusion has gained assent, men show no reluctance to accept the clear logical inferences following from the investigation of nature.

Among these results is *rejection of fixedness of species* as implying impossibility of deviation from a single normal type of structure. The possibility of adaptive changes being granted, the absolute fixedness of species in the rigid sense formerly acknowledged is abandoned. How great the modification of view must be, is much more difficult to decide, and hardly admits of exact statement. There is certainly no denial of distinction of species, nor can such denial ever find acceptance, whatever be the advance of theory, for the distinctions are so broad as to render this impossible. But the whole work of classification of the different orders of animal life, exceedingly difficult in any case, has been rendered much more perplexing in consequence of the accumulation of evidence favoring the doctrine of evolution. What can properly be regarded as the origin of a new species, and what as a mere modification or advance in a species already recognized, are questions for which it is difficult to find an exact answer. The theory of the "origin of species" by natural selection seems placed in an awkward perplexity as to what constitutes *origin* of a new order of life. And this difficulty must be regarded as a constant attendant on the scheme of thought, since "adaptive changes" must be of slow progress, and historically obscure, inasmuch as a succession of very slight differences must contribute to a general result. In this way it may even become matter of keen discussion what actually constitutes organic advance. Mr. Darwin admits serious difficulty at this point. He says, "Here we enter on a very intricate subject, for naturalists have not defined to each other's satisfaction what is meant by an advance in organization."* Thus there is dispute among competent authorities as to which may properly be considered the highest order of plants, and which the highest order of fishes. On the other hand, it is comparatively easy to decide among the more highly organized animals, when an advance is made, by reference to increased complexity in structure, or provision of separate organs for ac-

* *Origin of Species*, 4th ed. p. 141.

complishment of distinct functions. These considerations, however, suffice to indicate how many and complicated are the subjects requiring to be examined on evidence, and adjusted in their relations to each other, before it can be possible to get beyond surmise, in order to formulate a complete scientific theory. That "adaptive changes" by natural law of evolution are not only possible, but that they frequently occur under observation, admits of no question; but whether this includes changes of structure such as imply origin of species may still be subject of grave doubt. The alterations made by Mr. Darwin in successive editions of his book, from the first edition in 1859, to the sixth edition in 1872,* introduced, as he explains, "according as the evidence has become somewhat stronger or weaker," are sufficient to suggest that a vast amount of work remains to be done before a well-defined theory can be formulated. While there is universal agreement as to the possibility of "adaptive changes" to which Mr. Darwin provisionally restricted his theory on account of the investigations of

* It may be well to mention here that the *third* American edition is from the *fifth* English edition.

Nageli as to plants, and those of Broca as to animals, there is much diversity of opinion concerning the wider application of the theory of evolution. This diversity arises in part from the varying estimate of the value of evidence as now accumulated, and in part from the varying conception of the completeness of our records of the ancient history of organism as presented by geology. There is as yet no general consensus of opinion, nor is there likely to be for a long time to come. Mr. Darwin himself is sufficiently cautious and faithful to observational methods, to admit that there are serious difficulties, of some of which he ventures only to say that they "are greatly diminished," while some have disappeared. Other writers, such as Hæckel, with greatly less caution, and with much greater alacrity in leaping over chasms, are prepared to go much further and faster than Darwin. Many more are exceedingly doubtful as to the scientific value of the evidence at command, being, as Mr. Darwin has said, "much shaken in their former belief."* And of many it must be said that they are convinced that the evidence is far from warranting the con-

* *Origin of Species*, 6th ed., p. 289.

clusion that all organized existence can be traced to "only a few forms," or to "one," according to the alternatives suggested by Darwin in the closing sentence of his book.

Waiving, then, meanwhile, as the state of scientific evidence warrants us to do, the question of the probable number of primordial forms in which organized existence appeared, there is at least another definite result to be recorded as following from even a modified recognition of a theory of development, that is the *rejection of belief in the simultaneous origin of all species* or orders of animal life existing now in the world. The scientific conception of the history of animal life is, that there has been a historical progression in the appearance of animals, in so far as lower orders took precedence of higher, while the higher have shown large power of adaptation to the circumstances in which they have been placed. In accordance with the whole principles regulating the relations of religion and science, religious men, scientific and non-scientific, will readily acquiesce in this modification of general belief, as largely favored by evidence which geology supplies, and supported by testimony drawn from the actually existing order of things; and they will do so with clear recognition that this view involves no conflict with scriptural statement, and is so far from containing in it any thing antagonistic to the fundamental conception of the supernatural origin of existence, that it harmonizes with it, even intensifying the demand upon a transcendent cause for the rational explanation of the admitted order of things.

Having thus indicated in definite form the favorable impression made on the public mind by the theory of evolution under a law of natural selection, it will suffice to indicate very briefly the more prominent difficulties with which the theory has grappled, but from which it has not escaped. In doing so, it should be said that the careful and deliberate manner in which Mr. Darwin has faced the host of difficulties which have gathered around is deserving of highest praise, as in harmony with the scientific spirit, and in marked contrast with the light-and-go-easy style in which others, such as Hæckel, and even Schmidt, pass over the ground, announcing things as undoubted facts, and even "self-evident" truths, of which no man can speak with any degree of certainty. On the other hand, it seems a reasonable ground of complaint against many opponents of the theory, which Mr. Darwin urges specially against Mr. St. George Mivart, that it is no part of their plan "to give the various facts and considerations opposed to their own conclusions," while marshalling the difficulties against an evolution theory. And yet it should be remembered that a great service is done to science in a period of transition, when difficulties are powerfully urged against a popular hypothesis, as an injury is done to science by precipitate and ill-considered arguments in support of such a hypothesis.

Of the most serious difficulties in the way of a theory of descent by evolution, the *first* concerns *the nature of the evidence*, inasmuch as all change coming under observation does not indicate progression or improvement in the organism. The importance of this may be best indicated by quoting Mr. Darwin's explanatory words as to alterations in the fifth edition of his book on species. He says, "In the earlier editions of my *Origin of Species*, I probably attributed too much to the action of natural selection or survival of the fittest.

I have altered the fifth edition of the *Origin* so as to confine my remarks to adaptive changes of structure. I had not formerly sufficiently considered the existence of many structures, which appear to be, as far as we can judge, neither beneficial nor injurious, and this I believe to be one of the greatest oversights as yet detected in my work." When it is certain that deviation from the normal structure may take place which is a disadvantage to the individual, and that this may descend to offspring; when it is also shown that deviation may occur which appears to serve no end, that is, contributes to no phase of functional activity; when besides advantages gained are lost, and the race returns to its original type of structure; and when farther there are examples of degeneration, as in parasitic races,—such facts interpose special difficulties in the way of an all-embracing theory of progress by natural selection. Besides, as deviations occur of an unfavorable kind among domesticated animals under the care of man, it becomes obvious that progress may be readily lost even in most favorable circumstances.

The next outstanding difficulty is that of *meeting the requirements of logical inference.*

This has been specially urged by Mr. Mivart as bearing upon the "incipient stages" of advance, and the difficulty certainly presses heavily at that point. Natural selection may account for much in the history of higher organisms where powers of sensibility and locomotion are great, but how can we find in natural selection an adequate explanation of progress in organisms within which these powers are at the lowest. The difficulty is to get a cause sufficient to account for the start of a movement so vast as that which is to culminate in man. Mr. Darwin feels the force of this difficulty, and replies thus, "as we have no facts to guide us, speculation on the subject is almost useless."* But this perplexity which is most glaring at the beginning of the upward course, clings to the theory at every stage in the combination of struggle and improvement,—descent involving a real *ascent.* Whether the organism be more or less complex, it depends upon *external causes* for its improvement, and the dependence continues at every stage. Granting that there is everywhere struggle for existence and survival of the fittest, are these sufficient to account for

* *Origin of Species,* 6th. ed. chap. iv. p. 100.

results so great as are involved in unceasing advance of organism?

If it be argued that they are sufficient, a serious perplexity comes from the opposite quarter,—How does it happen that all organic existence does not advance together to a common elevation? If the theory accounts for advance, how shall we account for the want of it? The difficulties are as great for the theory in view of the large body of facts it does not attempt to include, as in the facts it strives to embrace. Agassiz put this difficulty with much force in 1857, and it has not received any satisfactory answer. He said, "It is a fact which seems to be entirely overlooked by those who assume an extensive influence of physical causes upon the very existence of organized beings, that the most diversified types of animals and plants are everywhere found under identical circumstances."* If, as Mr. Darwin says, "looking to the first dawn of life," we may believe that "all organic beings presented the simplest structure"; if the struggle for existence is uniformly en-

* *Contributions to the Natural History of the United States*, Introduction, Boston, 1857; and *Essay on Classification*, p. 15, published separately; London, 1859. See Appendix VI.

countered and leads to survival of the fittest, how is it that within the same area, organism has not advanced to similar complexity? If under constraint of the evidence for the theory, we surrender the doctrine of inevitable fixedness of species, how shall we nevertheless account for the permanence of species? It is not suggested that there is at successive stages "new and simple forms continually being produced by spontaneous generation." This hypothesis of Lamark is rejected by Mr. Darwin,* as it is by almost all scientific observers? How, then, can we explain the facts? We are told that certain orders have "fallen out" in the march of progress; but we need a scientific account of this which shall harmonize with a theory of action of environment, and such an account is not forthcoming. It may be said that the very success of the theory by accumulation of most striking and important evidence, is bringing it into difficulty, and suggesting its insufficiency. The more powerful and imposing the action of the law of natural selection, the more pressing becomes the need for a scientific explanation, at once distinct and harmonious, which will

* *Origin*, 4th ed. p. 143.

account for the persistence of species, when struggle for existence goes on under similar or even analogous action of environment. The presence everywhere of these lower forms alongside of the higher, adds greatly to the attractiveness of nature, and not even the grandeur of a universal advance towards the higher levels of organization would make up for the disappearance of the marvels of lower orders of animals. A monotony of grandeur may compare unfavorably with the wealth of variety and adversity; and so a law of continuity or persistence may be found adding to the greatness of a universe in which a law of progress or evolution also finds uniform application.

Upon this contrast between persistence and progress, general attention will henceforth be concentrated in judging of the place and value of a theory of descent. There is no need for hurry or impatience in this matter. The words of Mr. Darwin will find ready assent as he says, "No one ought to feel surprise at much yet remaining unexplained on the origin of species, if we make due allowance for our profound ignorance on the mutual relations of the inhabitants of the world at the present time, and still more during past ages."* In accordance with this acknowledgment, a wide range of scientific research still remains to be undertaken, and religious thought can have nothing but friendly interest in the work, as it may well be assured of drawing thence fresh contributions of great value for higher speculation concerning the government of the universe.

* *Origin of Species*, 6th. ed. chap. iv. p. 100

LECTURE V.

RELATIONS OF LOWER AND HIGHER ORGANISMS.

FROM the general aspects of the theory of species, we pass to the consideration of distinct groups of organism, with the view of ascertaining their relations to each other. In doing so, it is better to begin at the lower end of the scale, leaving for a more advanced stage of inquiry the higher types of organism. In this department of the subject, special obligations are due to the wide range of investigations either occasioned or stimulated by the theory of evolution. For, whatever may be the ultimate award passed on this theory, there will be a unanimous recognition of the great válue to science attending on the varied forms of inquiry stimulated by the writings of Mr. Charles Darwin. And one obvious and strong reason for such acknowledgment is that so many of the results of these researches have an inherent value quite distinct from their testimony in favor of the theory that the struggle for existence is the principal factor in the origin of new species.

One of the most interesting fields of observation thus opened, is that concerned with the fertilization of plants by the intervention of insects and birds. A beginning in this department was made by the German naturalist, Christian Konrad Sprengel, who published in 1793 the report of his observations. In this he has been followed by Darwin, in 1862; by Dr. Hooker, Professor Asa Gray whose contributions appeared in the *American Journal of Science and Art* in 1862, and 1863, Moggridge, Fritz Müller, and Sir John Lubbock. The facts now accumulated, rank as an important contribution to botany and zöology, and naturally fall within the circle of recent advances to which it is desirable that attention be turned.

The general result is one of great interest, as illustrating a striking degree of interdependence between lower and higher organisms, — the vegetable and animal kingdom contributing to each other's subsistence and propagation. Flowers present special attractions to insects flying around, alluring them by varied colors, and providing for them by secreting stores of honey; on the other hand, these insects (flies, bees, wasps, etc.), seeking the honey which satisfies their wants, at the same time carry the pollen from one flower to another, thus providing for the fertilizing of the plants. In some cases, fertilization is secured by a natural process within the organism itself; in other cases, the pollen is scattered over a region by the wind; but the most wonderful, and at the same time efficient mode of providing for the growth of vigorous plants, is fertilization by the agency of insect life.

A brief outline of the ordinary structure of the flower will introduce to a ready appreciation of the scientific interest attaching to this last mode of fertilization, both as concerning the functions of different portions of the flowers, and the relation of dependence established between higher and lower forms of organism, so that each is dependent on the other.

Every flower as it unfolds from the bud, consists of a series of whorls, or layers of substance twined or twirled round in such a manner as to unfold or coil back, as the flower opens. The *outermost* of these whorls (*calyx*) is a mere covering or sheath, usually of a green color, which protects the bud during the more tender period, curling up and withering as the flower opens, spreading forth its beauty. The *second* whorl (*corolla*) is what we more commonly regard as the flower proper, the colored leaves, or cup, or bell, according to the specific shape distinguishing the plant. The *third* whorl consists of a series of stalks or filaments (*stamens*) which as the flower matures or ripens stand up distinct from each other, each one having at its summit a little tuft or cushion (*anther*) covered with a fine dust or powder (*pollen*). The *fourth* or innermost whorl, the centre piece of the flower (*pistil*) is that in which the seed is generated and brought to maturity. We may thus say of the flower, that its outermost whorl is a temporary covering which withers and shrinks out of view, when the beauty of the inner structure is laid open; that the second is that which attracts the eye by the loveliness of its hues; while the two which belong to the internal structure of the flower are concerned with the reproduction or propagation of the plant, providing for the healthy germ from which a fresh plant of the same order may spring up. The relation of the fine yellow powder produced at the tips of the third whorl, to the seeds which are gathered together within the fourth whorl, is the matter to which special attention has been directed by the recent discoveries which have rewarded patient research. The fine powder or pollen needs to be carried to the seed, so that its properties may operate upon that seed, if it is to be fertilized, or so matured, as to fulfil its function in generating a new plant when it is committed to the soil. In many cases it is enough that the fine powder should fall down from its elevation on the seeds below. This is self-fertilization, and is easily provided for by the mere bending of the head of the flower as it approaches maturity, or by the swaying of it in the breeze. But a more difficult, and as we might be inclined to add, more precarious, because less certain, method for fertilization is required in many cases. The experiments carried on by all our gardeners, and in a still more extended scale in all our centres of botanic research, have established the fact that in many cases, the yellow powder of one plant must be in some manner carried over to the seed produced within another flower, if that seed is to yield a satisfactory result to the horticulturist.

We have thus two prominent facts here. The one is *the essential importance of the pollen* for fertilization; and the other, *the need for the transference of the pollen* from one plant to another in order to secure reproduction of vigorous growth by the sowing of the seed. As to the first, the pollen, which appears a fine powder or flour contains fluid protoplasm, that which Professor Huxley has described as the "single physical basis of life under all the diversities of vital existence."* These pollen grains falling on the seed discharge their protoplasmic fluid upon it, and by this means contribute to fertilization. This original or primordial form of vitalising agency is carried from one part of the flower to another, and this transference is the law regulating the propagation of flowering plants.

But, just at this point, we come upon the most striking results of recent research. Though all pollen is of this primary nature, named protoplasm, it is not found to hold true that pollen is of the same value for fertilization from whatever quarter it comes.

* *Lay Sermons*, chap. vii., p. 134.

On the contrary, most important differences result according to the source of the pollen. There is first the process of self-fertilization. But in many cases,—Mr. Darwin has shown that this holds of the majority of the orchids, —transference of the pollen from one plant to another proves to be a great advantage, if not an actual necessity for propagation of the plant. This process, known as cross-fertilization, gives a healthy and vigorous growth; want of it, will lead to degeneration, and ultimate extinction. This discovery has introduced a whole series of the most striking observations, throwing a flood of light on the distribution and interdependence of distinct forms of organism. The necessary relation between the pollen and the seed having been acknowledged, and next the value of transference of pollen from one plant to another, the first step in the line of discovery was made by the observation of a natural provision to *prevent self-fertilization* by rendering it impossible that the pollen of a plant should fall on the seed of that plant. This entrance on the line of discovery was made by Sprengel so far back as 1790, by whom it was observed that in many plants the pollen and the seed did not come to ripeness at the same time.* In some cases, the pollen is ripened before the seeds are ready; in other cases, the order of events is reversed. This observation naturally suggested transference of pollen from one plant to another; and this, connected with the continual coming and going of flies, bees, and butterflies, led to the further discovery, that *insects* unwittingly perform a large part of the work needful in order to *provide for fertilization.* Mr. Darwin has pointed out that from the paper of Robert Brown in the *Linnean Transactions*, in 1833, and from that of Dr. Hooker in the *Philosophic Transactions* for 1854, the peculiar phenomena had begun to awaken scientific interest. It was, however, when the researches as to origin of species had given fresh motive to observation concerning the relations of different types of organism, that the whole facts were brought to view, separately recorded, and at length systematized so as to lead to their full interpretation. Mr. Darwin himself concentrated on the orchids as peculiarly interesting and suggestive, while a host of work-

* Darwin's *Fertilization of Orchids*, p. 2; Lubbock's *Scientific Lectures*, p. 8.

ers all over the world were turning their energies into this new field of observation which promised ample return for patient research.

As a reward of these investigations important facts have been established on ample evidence. First, it has been confirmed by varying lines of evidence that transference of pollen, or cross-fertilization, is of special value in the development of plant life. Investigation has strengthened the evidence of disadvantage arising from fertilization by exclusive dependence on self-produced pollen. Fritz Müller has recorded a variety of observations that the pollen of some flowers has so little influence on the seed produced on the same stem that when it falls upon the seeds no effect is produced; the pollen lies there as if possessed of no more vitalizing power than grains of dust. And, what is even more surprising, Müller has found examples in which the pollen does act upon the seeds of its own flower, but acts *injuriously*, insomuch that the flower, the pollen, and the seed-producing portion of the plant begin to decay.* So

* Sir John Lubbock's *Scientific Lectures*, p. 3. Mr. Darwin refers to Fritz Müller's papers as reported in *Botanische Zeitung*, 1869–70. Appendix IX.

deep has been the impression made on Mr. Darwin's mind by the evidence of provision for transference of pollen, that he closes his valuable and interesting book on the *Fertilization of Orchids* with the following statements. Having remarked that "self-fertilization would have been an incomparably safer and easier process than the transportal of pollen from flower to flower," he adds these words,—"It is hardly an exaggeration to say that Nature tells us, in the most emphatic manner, that she abhors perpetual self-fertilization." *

The next result secured presents an important relation between animal life and vegetable. These flowers do not depend for their fertilization upon the action of the wind, which in scattering profusely in all directions must occasion large waste of pollen. There is found to be distinct provision for carrying the pollen from one flower to another by insects, such as the bees, whose industry in gathering honey has been celebrated from ancient times, specially because of our interest in the store-house, but with little suspicion of the double work being done by

* *The Various Contrivances by which Orchids are fertilized by Insects*, 2d ed. p. 293.

the bees, who add to their other industry that of horticulturists. These bees are the pollen-bearers,—the recognized local carriers, regularly on the road,—doing the work which the flowers, in lack of locomotive power, could not do for each other. Or, looking at the relation of things from another point of view, the bees are at the same time gathering the honey, and sowing the seed for a future harvest. This reference to the honey, however, introduces to notice a companion series of facts, showing the provision in completed form for an interchange of services. The plants supply an attraction to the animals, while the animals render a service to the plants. This phase of interdependence is made more conspicuous by the contrast apparent in the structure and functions of plants fertilized by the wind, such as the larger shrubs and trees, which as they present a greater surface to the breeze, do not call for the same detailed provision for carrying the pollen. In contrast with these more bulky representatives of the vegetable kingdom, the more lowly and insignificant in size, as well as more short-lived, present many attractions in color, scent, and secretion of honey, all adapted to the nature of insects, suited for the work of pollen carrying. The attractions of form, color, and scent in the flowers are well known to us; but they are also appreciated by the insects,—a fact which may possibly suggest that a high degree of intellectual power is not required for appreciation of these qualities, as no one pro fesses that bees rank high intellectually. At the same time, if comparisons are to be made at this point, the farther suggestion may also be introduced, that there is little testimony to intelligence where search for food is concerned, and while the human race do not feed on flowers, insects are constantly feeding from them. The attractions in the two cases therefore vary considerably in their significance. Restricting attention, however, to the special field of observation now before us, with the view simply of ascertaining the relations of plants and insects, color and honey present the two most prominent attractions accounting for the perpetual hum of life heard amongst the flowering plants. Different parts of the flower provide for variegated coloring, and stores of honey; these present attractions to the insects; and the structure of the flowers as they provide for the landing of the insects, and require that they penetrate to their centre for the secreted honey, secures that the work needful for fertilization be effectually done. This last feature of adaptation is that on which attention may be specially concentrated here. Mr. Darwin in treating of orchids has described this part of their structure in these words;—"In almost all the species, one of the petals (or leaves of the flower) which is properly the upper one, is larger than the others and stands on the lower side of the flower, where it offers a landing-place for insects."* Towards the inner or root end of this leaf (*labellum*) is the gland, in some flowers appearing only as a slit, in others forming like a tube, (*nectary*) which secrets the honey. Just over the entrance to the part where the honey is to be found stands that which secrets the pollen prepared for fertilizing some other flower. So soon as the bee or other insect presses its head well into the centre of the flower, some of the pollen adheres to it; when the head is withdrawn, this pollen is borne off to the flower which the bee next visits; and as the

* *Fertilization*, p. 5.

head is pressed into the core of this flower the pollen is deposited, and provision for fertilization is complete. Special features appearing in certain classes of the orchids illustrate how it is possible for the bee so laden to visit many flowers without depositing the pollen, yet a little later accomplish the object quite simply. The following illustration from Mr. Darwin's account of the first orchid selected, will suffice. Just *above* the entrance to the honey store, lies a pouch connected with the pollen store. As the head of the bee is pressed down towards the honey, this pouch is burst open, and from it issues a little sticky gland or disc, or it may be two of these discs. These adhere at once to the head of the bee, and being connected by a slight band with packets of pollen grains so soon as the animal retires the pollen is drawn with it, standing out like a seed vessel on the head. The strangest part of the contrivance appears in what thereafter follows. "The viscid matter has the peculiar chemical quality, of setting like cement, hard and dry in a few minutes." Suppose both the little viscid balls have been withdrawn, the bands bearing the pollen will appear "projecting up like horns."

"How then can the flower be fertilized? This is effected by a beautiful contrivance; though the viscid surface remains immovably affixed, the apparently insignificant and minute disc of membrane to which the caudicle adheres is endowed with a remarkable power of contraction, which causes the pollinium to sweep through an angle of about ninety degrees, always in one direction towards the apex of the proboscis, in the course of thirty seconds on an average."* That is, the two erections bearing packets of pollen which formerly stood up almost perpendicular, like horns, begin to lower until they reach the horizontal; in this way when the bee enters a flower the packets of pollen inevitably touch the seed stores, communicating what is required for their fertilization. Nor have we even yet the whole of the contrivances adapted for this end. "Here comes into play another pretty adaptation." The seed vessel to be fertilized is very sticky, "but not so viscid as when touched by a pollinium to pull the whole off an insect's head." But it is sufficiently adhesive "to break the elastic threads by which the packets of pollen grains are tied together." In this way, it

* *Fertilization*, p. 12.

tears off so much from the store adhering to the head of the bee, and still leaves there what may supply the requirements of many flowers besides. The description thus given will suffice to indicate how close is the relation of the lower orders of animal life with vegetable life, and will illustrate how the lower organism may be dependent for existence on the higher, an illustration in some respect the converse of the facts illustrating origin of species by development.

There remains in this department of inquiry only one additional set of facts, to which reference may be made, as illustrating *distribution of work among insects and birds*, assigning them to different orders of plants. This will illustrate contrivance on a still wider scale, discovering distinct sets of affinity, which imply common localization for given plants and animals. In this it appears that flies, humble bees, and birds with long slender bills, such as the humming birds, all have a share in the work required for fertilizing plants.

There is one example, *epipactis latifolia*, with a cup-shaped labellum, in which honey is secreted, and which bees are never seen to frequent. What, however, the bees pass, the wasps suck eagerly, and by them it is fertilized. Of this flower, Mr. Darwin says,—"It is very remarkable that the sweet nectar of this *epipactis* should not be attractive to any kind of bee. If wasps were to become extinct in any district, so probably would the *Epipactis Latifolia.*"*

Another example there is of an orchid (*Spiranthes Autumnalis*), commonly known as *Ladies' Tresses*, having a series of spikes, of which the lowest flowers are first matured, the others following in order as they rise towards the summit. This plant is frequented by bees, whose practice it is to begin with the lowest flowers and ascend gradually to the top. This order in seeking to extract the honey, proves to be the proper one for fertilizing of the plant, because the pollen which the bee brings will be received by the riper flower on which it lands, and when that has been deposited, fresh pollen will adhere to the bee as it rises to the less matured flowers, and thus it departs laden with pollen destined for the lowest flowers of the next plant it visits.†

These examples introduce us to a general plan for fertilization of plants by the inter-

* *Fertilization*, p. 102. † *Ib.* p. 113.

vention of insects, so complete in the order of distribution that we may classify the plants according to the insect by which they are fertilized, making it natural to speak of fly orchids, spider orchids, wasp orchids, and bee orchids. In all cases the search for honey determines the visits made, leaving still unexplained, however, the fact that the nectar of some plants is shunned by certain insects, and eagerly absorbed by others. With the general source of attraction in the flowering plants, there are diversities of arrangement among the insects, according to the comparative size of the flower, and strength required in order to penetrate to the inner chamber where the honey is stored. Because of the minuteness of the aperture, there are flowers from which the bee can not draw supplies; on the other hand, because of the size and strength of the flower, there are cases in which the ordinary bee is incapable of reaching the store, and the stronger humble bee alone succeeds in effecting an entrance.

There is thus presented in mere outline a general view of the interdependence of lower and higher orders of organism. While each flower develops pollen and seed, there are arrangements connected with the ripening of these two, which restrain or even prevent self-fertilization. Along with this there are distinct lines of evidence to establish the rule that cross-fertilization, or transference of pollen from one flower to the seed of another, secures the growth of a much healthier and more vigorous order. Where such transference is provided for otherwise than by the wind, the attractiveness of the flowers brings to them at the proper season, the insects which carry the pollen, and to each class of insect is distributed a distinct share in the work. In these facts we have a natural law for preservation of species, discovering in a very striking manner the dependence of lower organism on higher. As Mr. Darwin has said,—"The *meaning* of these facts is clear." Referring to the examples in which the insects have to bore holes in order to reach the honey, where there is need for time to allow for the hardening of the viscid matter, he has used the following words which are most fitly applied,—"If this double relation is accidental, it is a fortunate accident for the plants; but I can not believe it to be so, and it appears to me one of the most wonderful cases of adaptation which has ever been recorded." * It is most obviously true, as Sir John Lubbock has said, that "neither plants nor insects would be what they are, but for the influence which each has exercised on the other." † In view of the facts here very briefly described it will generally be allowed that Mr. Darwin's expectation from the study of orchids will be verified,—"An examination of their many beautiful contrivances will exalt the whole vegetable kingdom in most persons' estimation." ‡ We have enough before us to enable us to appreciate our author's feeling when he says, "Hardly any fact has struck me so much as the endless diversities of structure,—the prodigality of resources for gaining the very same end." § Again when giving us his prevailing impression he says,—"The more I study nature, the more I become impressed with ever-increasing force, that the contrivances and beautiful adaptations, slowly acquired through each part occasionally varying in a slight degree, but in many ways, with the preservation of those variations which were beneficial to the organism under complex and

* *Fertilization*, p. 44. † *Scientific Lectures*, p. 31.
‡ *Fertilization*, p. 2. § *Ib.* p. 284.

ever varying conditions of life, transcend in an incomparable manner the contrivances and adaptations which the most fertile imagination of man could invent." *

In preparing the present summary of recent advances in this department of natural history, I have resorted freely to quotation, because of the obvious rule, that it is better for scientific interest, for proper understanding, and for regulation of all subsequent reasoning on the facts, that we have the observations presented as nearly as possible by those who made them, and that we have more general inferences in the very words of those whose minds have been filled and swayed by impressions made in the field of observation itself. In now proceeding to consider the bearing of these advances on religious thought, I shall keep as far as possible by the same rule, desiring that science may interpret itself, and translate its own special conclusions into their fit place within a scheme of the universe. And whatever there may be here of material for detailed inference, it will be taken by religious men as abundantly clear, that science in slowly unfolding to general view

* *Fertilization.* p. 285.

these secrets of nature, renders a lasting and most valuable service to religion. Our religious convictions and emotions rest on a wider intellectual basis according to the fulness with which we understand the marvels of adaptation and contrivance which lie covered from ordinary observation under the attractive surface of nature.

Altogether beyond such a general admission as this, however, it must be obvious that in the mass of deeply interesting material now before us, there lies a considerable number of truths needing to be gathered into generalized form, bearing upon the laws of nature applying to living organism. As records of details are extended before us, the marvels of structure are obvious. The multifarious contrivances become quite startling, until we are ready to lose our reckoning in the very multiplicity of facts narrated. In order to make sure of general result, we need to draw off somewhat from details,—to be content even to lose sight of many of them,—in order to gain a position, sufficiently removed for a sight of general relations. In attempting this it is clear that there are certain truths bearing on the preservation and development of species in the vegetable kingdom, and an analogous set of truths as to the animal kingdom, and above these, possibly still more important for general appreciation of the universe as a whole, a body of truth as to the relations of plants and animals.

As to the first of these, it seems obvious that within the single field of observation presented by orchids,—comparatively narrow, in view of the wide domain of the vegetable kingdom, and yet astonishingly extensive, on account of the richness of detail,—there is a large body of evidence to support the theory of origin of species by selection and adaptation. Whether all the orchideæ now found in existence have sprung from one order of plant, or from several, the testimony appears ample to support at least the following conclusion as presented in the words of Mr. Darwin, "that the now wonderfully changed structure of the flower is due to a long course of slow modification,—each modification having been preserved which was useful to the plant, during the incessant changes to which the organic and inorganic world has been exposed."*

* *Fertilization*, p. 246.

By a line of inference exactly similar, a like conclusion must be reached as to insect life. For, important as the observations are, bearing on the transference of pollen from the place where it is generated to the place where it is wanted, we must notice that the whole work is done in consequence of search for honey by flies, moths, ants, wasps, and bees. It naturally follows that all these insects have been going through some measure of adaptation, as well as the plants. The same law must have been operating in their history while prosecuting the unceasing search for food. It may be exceedingly difficult to fill up the line of progress, or trace the causes in operation, which could favor the conclusion that all the insects named have sprung from a common stock. Still more perplexing might it be to maintain the argument that these very insects have sprung according to a sure law of descent, from vegetable life itself. But there is ample evidence to warrant the inference that in length of proboscis, formation of limbs, and other features in their structure, modifications have resulted from the struggle needful to reach the nectar secreted in the flowers.

But it is clearly impossible to stop here in our inferences. There is interdependence of lower and higher organisms, to which a distinct place needs to be assigned in our theory of the universe. Even if it be granted, as it readily will be by those who have studied the results of recent research, that there is a vast body of evidence to prove that there is development of species by adaptation and selection, it is equally evident that this is not the only law affecting the existence of different orders of organized beings. Just as clear as it is that pollen and seed are both required to provide for the continuance of plant life, so clear is it that plants are needed to support insects, and insects to propagate plants. Proceeding on the same lines of reasoning as have been already employed, we must inquire how this interdependence is to be accounted for under natural law? The struggle for existence is clearly performing an important part in the development of plants, and also of animals; and so long as we regard these two orders singly, it seems obvious how changes in structure may be accounted for; but observations have become so interlaced, that a new problem has been raised in connection with facts manifestly abating the struggle for existence. In view of this problem Dr. Hooker has said,—"The adjustment of the parts of the flower to the form and habits of the insect or bird, and of these to the flower, is so accurate, that it is in vain to speculate whether the plant was adapted to feed the animal, or the animal adapted to fertilize the plant."* This suggestion of the needlessness of speculation is natural from a scientific point of view, and we may do well to remember the warnings against risks attending the search for final causes, which have been sounded from the days of Spinoza to the present time; but there is a problem here which science can not leave in abeyance. The facts are undoubted, and the natural causes must be sought. The parts of the flowers are adapted to the forms and habits of the insects; the insects are adapted to the work of fertilizing the plants; the question is, How are these two things secured? The inquiry which has awakened general interest as to the development of species in the history of distinct orders such as orchids, insects, pig-

* *Botany*, (Science Primers) by Dr. J. D. Hooker, C.B., P.R.S., p. 79.

eons, and dogs, must strive to complete its work, by pressing on to this more complicated question concerning the adaptation of distinct organisms to influence and aid each other in the work of development. In what way science may deal with this question, and how far it may be able to advance in the search for an answer, it may be difficult to decide. For it is much easier to indicate the logical necessity for an advance, than to say in what manner the advance is to be accomplished. The one is a simple question of logical requirement; the other must be a matter of continued observation, and scientific inference. Whether science may yet discover an answer; or whether it may prove true at this point, as at other points already mentioned, that science has here reached clear marks of its own limits, must be left to the future, to be determined by those devoted to scientific research. As long, however, as this question of interdependence remains without a scientific explanation, it must be obvious that there are important facts which seem to imply some modification of the theory of descent, or evolution of species by means of selection, under the severe struggle for existence. Or, to put it from another point of view, nature has marvellously provided for mitigation of the struggle for existence, by contrivances providing both for vegetable and animal life; therefore the theory of the origin and development of life which depends chiefly on the struggle for existence must be adjusted to allow for a theory of the effects arising from the natural provision for obviating the struggle, and providing for a large increase of life.

Quite beyond this, as a matter entirely distinct, is the question as to the primordial forms of existence in the history of plants and insects. As to this, science may be able to give very little testimony, as it is a question of the remote past, on which present facts may afford little evidence. Still, beyond these primordial forms, in a region which science can not enter, there lies the question of origin, of actual beginning, creation of life, as to the reality of which science can speak only indirectly by discovery of its own limits, in the terms of its *ultimatum*, nature has provided that such and such things shall be.

Before leaving the department of insect life, there is a collateral and complementary series of observations, bearing upon the nature and activity of ANTS, which deserves attention. The ants are a race of insects as diligently industrious as the bees, like them also fond of honey and of all sweet substances; but unlike them ready to devour other insects. Along with the industry of the bee, they have predatory tendencies, leading them into conflict with other races, or even involving different orders of their own race in warfare. It is a curious fact, in this connection, that many of the flowering plants have contrivances which guard them from the approach of ants. Creeping insects find the way barred against them, while the flying insect at once and easily reaches the stores of honey, not knowing any thing of the difficulties in the path of the less favored rival. Spikes grow with their points in a downward direction, against which no creeping insect can make way; waxy or glutinous matter is spread over the leaves, which insects shun as a trap; and there are velvety flexible leaves from the edge of which the insect easily slips off. Special attention has been turned to this field of research by Kerner,* an interesting outline of the results of

* *Flowers and their Unbidden Guests*, by Prof. Kerner, University of Innsbruck.

his observations being given by Sir John Lubbock.* The conclusion reached as to the utility of these contrivances for exclusion of creeping insects, is that they perform an auxiliary part in the general plan for fertilization which has been described. To allow the store of honey to go to the ants would be merely to feed them without any equivalent advantage to the flowers. To diminish the supply in this way, might cause the bees to abandon many flowers, and so greatly diminish fertilization. This would ultimately lead to short supplies, and probable extinction of several orders of plants and animals, and accordingly these contrivances to hinder the access of ants, must be added to those for facilitating the approach of bees, and other flying insects, affording further evidence of the adjustment of rival interests involved in the relations of the vegetable and animal kingdoms. The serried spikes are a phalanx of bayonets planted for resistance of an advancing foe.

Contemplating now the ants as in some respects an excluded race, which with a large share of pugnacity can not find a basis of operations for contending against the bees, we

* *Scientific Lectures*, p. 36.

have to turn attention briefly on their modes of life. The industry of the ant is proverbial, and can not fail to arrest the attention of any one who spends a few minutes before an ant-hill. But carefully recorded observations prove it to be much greater than could have been imagined. Sir John Lubbock has rendered special service here by carefully noting the time occupied, as well as the amount of work done, thus preserving a series of observations exceedingly suggestive in many ways, and having an important bearing on a considerable number of difficult questions connected with the relative powers of lower and higher orders of life. A similar service has been rendered in America in the work of the Rev. H. C. McCook of Philadelphia, on *The Natural History of the Agricultural Ant of Texas*, —a book recording careful and most important observations, adding much to the stores of knowledge concerning ants.*

The work of the ants is directed mainly to the two great objects of animal life, procuring food, and caring for the young, to which falls to be added, the repelling of attacks upon their nests, or removal of any thing obnoxious. They destroy great numbers of smaller

* See Appendix X.

insects, bearing them to their nests for consumption, besides going off in search of honey which may be within reach, and not guarded with spikes. This mode of providing implies a very busy life, and they do not as a rule grudge work. Besides procuring supplies, however, there is a large amount of labor in the care bestowed upon their young. Without attempting to distinguish various orders, of which "more than seven hundred kinds are known," * a general description of their young will suffice. In the earliest stage of their existence, the larvæ are small conical shaped grubs, without power of movement. In this state they are fed, carried about from place to place as if their seniors were seeking change of air and temperature for them; and in process of these removals and arrangements, they are often grouped together in separate companies, and in exact order according to their size. In their next stage, they become pupæ, sometimes quite exposed, in other cases covered with a thin silken covering. From this, they pass into the mature state as perfect insects, and in process of this transition older ants render assistance by way of aiding the transition, "carefully

* See Appendix VIII.

unfolding their legs and smoothing out their wings."

In the ant nest there is a singular distinction of orders which prevents us speaking of the *parent* ants as doing all this work for the young. The great majority in every nest are neuters, not producing young; these are the workers, and they are destitute of wings. The smaller numbers only are the males and females producing the young. The workers, shorn of wings, and entrusted with all that is required in household and out-door duties, labor assiduously. These neuter ants have occasioned special perplexity to Mr. Darwin as bearing on the theory of evolution, a difficulty which is seriously increased by the fact that in some cases they "differ from each other, sometimes to an almost incredible degree, and are thus divided into two or even three castes," and these "do not commonly graduate into each other," but are "as distinct from each other as any two species."* Without following Mr. Darwin through his reasoning as to the adaptation of neuters for their task in life, it may be well to quote his words towards its close, where he says, "I

* *Origin of Species*, 6th ed. p. 230.

must confess, that, with all my faith in natural selection, I should never have anticipated that this principle could have been efficient in so high a degree, had not the case of these neuter insects led me to this conclusion."* Besides the fact that these neuters are the workers, there is an additional circumstance, established by Mr. Frederick Smith by observations in England, confirmed by the observations of Pierre Huber in Switzerland, and afterwards verified in the clearest way by Mr. Darwin, that there is a species of ant (*formica sanguinea*) which captures slaves of a weaker order, making war against the weaker race, carrying off their young, rearing them within their own nests, and training them to serve. Mr. Darwin was himself sceptical of such a statement, but gives an interesting narrative of distinct observations by which it was confirmed.

The amount of labor undertaken by the workers from an ants' nest, may be judged by one or two extracts from the records of Sir John Lubbock. He says, "I once watched an ant from six in the morning, and she worked without intermission till a quarter

* *Origin of Species,* 6th ed. p. 233.

to ten at night," and in that time she had carried one hundred and eighty-seven larvæ into the nest.* There is evidence not only of coöperation, but of division of labor among the workers. The observations of Mr. Forel lead to the conclusion that "very young ants devote themselves at first to the care of the larvæ and pupæ, and that they do not take share in the defence of the nest or other out-of-door work, until they are some days old."† By a distinct set of observations, watching all ants that came and went from the nest, and laying up in captivity some of the number, Mr. Lubbock came to the conclusion "that certain ants are told off as foragers."‡ And in the winter season, when in the case of some orders little food is required, a few only of the inhabitants of the nest come and go, for the purpose of carrying in supplies. This makes observation much more easy at that season, rendering it possible to number and identify individual workers. The results as applicable to one of the nests are given in the following sentences. "From the 1st of November to the 5th of January, with two or three casual exceptions, the whole of the supplies were car-

* *Scient. Lects.* p. 73. † *Ib.* p. 78. ‡ *Ib.* p. 135.

ried in by three ants, one of whom, however, did comparatively little. The other two were imprisoned, and then, but not till then, a fresh ant appeared on the scene. She carried in the food for a week, and then she being imprisoned, two others undertook the task." *

One consideration more bearing upon obtaining supplies deserves to be recorded as altogether singular. Some species of ants watch over a distinct order of insects, the aphides, which exude a sweet fluid, using them exactly as we do cows for obtaining supplies of milk. The ant comes up to the aphis, gently strokes it with her feelers, forthwith the aphis gives forth its supply of honey, which the ant drinks up and departs. The facts were observed by Pierre Huber, and verified by Mr. Darwin. This verification was so interesting, that I give the narrative in a slightly condensed form. Mr. Darwin says,—"I removed all the ants from a group of about a dozen aphides on a dock-plant, and prevented their attendance during several hours." Mr. Darwin tried in vain by stroking the aphides with a hair, in imitation of the play of the feelers of the ants, to induce them to give up the

* *Scientific Lectures*, p. 135.

honey. "Afterwards," he says, "I allowed an ant to visit them, and it immediately seemed, by its eager way of running about, to be well aware what a rich flock it had discovered; it then began to play with its antennæ on the abdomen first of one aphis and then of another; and each, as soon as it felt the antennæ, immediately lifted up its abdomen and excreted a limpid drop of sweet juice, which was eagerly devoured by the ant."* So the ants have their "cows" and milk them.

To attempt any account of the ants of tropical countries, where ants are most numerous, swarming in the regions they inhabit, and marching in hosts, would occupy too much space. I give, therefore, only a single reference extracted from the testimony of Mr. Savage concerning the driver ant of Western Africa (*Anomma Arcens*), so called because of the success with which it drives every thing before it. Mr. Savage annoyed by the proximity of a large settlement, discovered its quarters in some decaying granite. Kindling a fire around it, he believed he had succeeded in disposing of that settlement. Two days after, he went back to the spot, and instead

* *Origin of Species* 6th ed. p. 207.

of desolation and death, he found "a tree at a short distance, about eighteen inches in diameter, to the height of four feet from the ground, with the adjacent plants and earth perfectly black with them." The most striking thing, however, was that the ants had made festoons from the lower branches to the ground, formed in the following manner, as witnessed by Mr. Savage: "ant after ant coming down from above, extending their long limbs, and opening wide their jaws, gradually lengthening out the living chain" until first it was swaying to and fro, and ultimately fastened to the ground, when "others were ascending and descending upon them, thus holding free and ready communication with the lower and upper portions of this dense mass." In this same manner these ants provide for the crossing of water when on the march. "They make a line or chain of one another, gradually extending themselves by numbers across till the opposite side is reached."* This is exactly similar to the manner in which some monkeys are known to construct a natural bridge, only that the monkeys have the ad-

* *Museum of Natural History* edited by Richardson, Dallas, Cobbold, Baird, and White, vol. ii. p. 184.

vantage of greater size and muscular strength, as well as prehensile power by the use of their tails. With such characteristics as have been briefly described, there is little wonder that a high place in the scale of intelligence has been claimed for these small insects. Sir John Lubbock, who has so patiently conducted his observations as to their modes of life, has stated this in the following manner,—"The anthropoid apes no doubt approach more to man in bodily structure than do any other animals; but when we consider the habits of ants, their social organization, their large communities, elaborate habitations, their roadways, their possession of domestic animals, and even in some cases of slaves, it must be admitted that they have a fair claim to rank next to man in the scale of intelligence."* Whether, even with all this evidence, we may be able to rank the ants quite as high as Lubbock here suggests, may be open to question. There may, for example, be reasonable debate whether the dog does not present still higher signs of intelligence, but it says a great deal for the ants that debate in the case should be possible. A question of very great scientific im-

* *Scient. Lects.* p. 68.

portance is here raised, affecting the whole scheme of interpretation applicable to animal life, as connected with development of brain.

Without attempting to enter upon the argument yet to be conducted through the wider relations concerned, it must be obvious that the facts bearing on insect life must erelong have a larger share than they have yet had in influencing our generalizations. By reference to these, it becomes apparent, that anatomical structure is not in itself an adequate guide in determining comparative importance on the scale of organic existence; and, what is still more startling, that even comparative brain structure can not be taken as the sole test of the measure of intelligence belonging to animals. The whole orders of ants, taken collectively, must be regarded as presenting quite exceptional difficulties, not only for a theory of evolution regarded as an all-embracing science of life; but also for that theory of intelligence which seeks to account for diversities of power by the comparative complexity of brain structure.

Passing from more detailed discussion, it is needful to observe how wide and valuable are the results of these researches concerning the relation of the vegetable kingdom with lower orders of animals. Facts now recorded in multitudes of scientific journals, and more elaborate treatises, illustrate wonderful minuteness of contrivance and completeness of adaptation in the works of nature, giving to the range of knowledge possessed only a century ago an aspect of insignificance. What the microscope has done by enlarging the range of human vision, subdivision of labor among scientific inquirers, and proportionate concentration, have done, in the way of embracing the vast and complicated field of observation lying open to all eyes. The results exalt to a greatly higher place in our appreciation the evidence of design in the world. The consequence is that while the line of thought followed by Paley, in what he designated *Natural Theology*, has become a thousand-fold more interesting, the familiar and now almost antiquated illustration of the *watch*, taken as a model of human design, by the comparative simplicity of its adjustments, seems strangely inadequate to represent even in the most temporary form, a minuteness of design quite overwhelming to the human mind in its attempts to bring it within a uniform scheme.

LECTURE V.

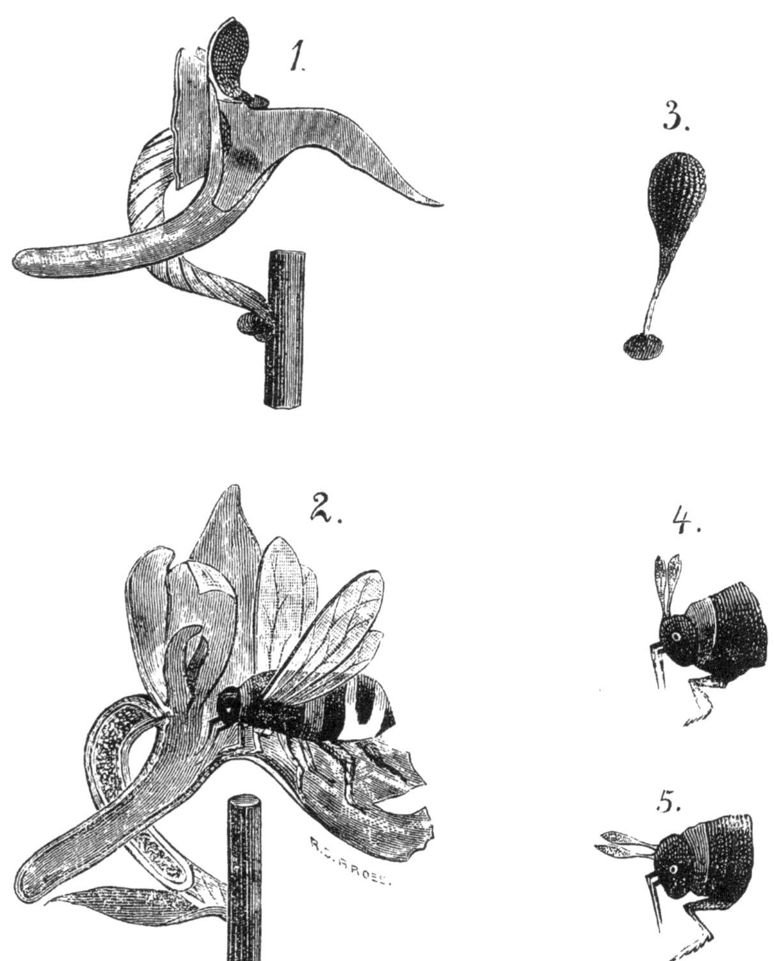

1. Section of Orchid Flower, showing pollen vessel, seed store, and honey store. 2. Bee entering. 3. Pollen vessel. 4. Bee retreating. 5. Bee prepared for entering another flower.

Whether all this was provided for by manifold creative acts, or by development from a few primordial forms, does not affect the argument; the latter suggestion only greatly increases its force. To those who are swayed only by an intellectual interest, the facts of vegetable and insect life must be full of significance, suggestive of far-reaching reflection. But to no body of men can these results of scientific research be so attractive as to those who require for all nature a supernatural explanation.

LECTURE VI.

HIGHER ORGANISMS.—RESEMBLANCES AND CONTRASTS.—BRAIN STRUCTURE.

THE stage of investigation now reached requires us to consider recent advances in our knowledge of more complicated organisms. This leads into the line of observation disclosing steadily advancing complexity of structure, and brings us into contact with the claim that man be included within the area of scientific inquiry, and regarded as a more fully organized life to which lower orders are not only pointing, but actually tending.

As to this last claim, about which more must be said as we approach the close of these investigations, it may be remarked by way of preliminary, that as man belongs to nature, all the characteristics of his life must come within the area of scientific inquiry, and indeed the test of any theory of existence which may be offered, will be found in the measure of success with which it explains our own nature. That man stands highest in the scale of organism belonging to this world admits of no doubt, therefore the explanation of human nature may be regarded as the supreme effort of science. Around this subject, however, serious differences have arisen among scientific men, but these differences do not concern the very simple question whether all that belongs to nature comes within the range of the science of nature. This is granted by all, whether there be a preference for including all such inquiry under the single name of science, or for distinguishing between physical science and mental philosophy. This is simply a matter of defining terms, and tracing the boundaries of recognized departments of inquiry. But whether a continued study of organism will conduct us to an adequate understanding of human nature, must be a matter of observation and inference. If it do, science has completed its work. If it do not, there remains a still higher question, how shall we account for features of life for which organism affords no scientific explanation? The whole field is certainly free to science, and the whole task which this immense field of research imposes must be undertaken, and persistently prosecuted to a rational issue.

Entering now, therefore, on the contemplation of animal life, regarded as a higher order, distinguishable from vegetable life, we have the outstanding characteristics of sensibility and locomotion. Whether there is a distinct line of demarcation between vegetable and animal does not require special attention, for no matter of controversy on this point can delay procedure. There is, as already remarked, in the vegetable kingdom a singular approximation towards animal life, in so far as we have evidence of sensibility to touch among the plants, to a degree which appears wonderful chiefly by contrast with the common characteristics of the vegetable kingdom. On the other hand, sensibility to influences operating from without is a common feature of animal life. Even the very lowest orders of animals are sensitive to touch, and as this form of experience is closely connected with power of locomotion, all animals have the conditions of their life largely affected by interference with their own movements, or resistance offered, whether by objects lying in their way, or by some force restraining their progress, or causing movement in an opposite direction. Now these two characteristics—sensibility to impression from without, and movement caused by an exercise of energy from within the organism itself—are both provided for by means of the nerve system belonging to the animal. This nerve system varies in the number and complexity of its arrangements, according to the complexity of the organism with which it is associated. As, therefore, we rise in the scale, passing from the soft pulpy form of the lowest orders, to those formed in segments or rings, next to those with distinct portions of organism fulfilling separate functions, as in insect life, with head, body, and legs; and next pass up to the vertebrates, with back-bone and skeleton, on which is built up a more or less complicated muscular system, we find a nerve system, growing in complexity along with the appearance of different organs of the body. And in all cases, this system fulfils these two functions—sensibility to touch, and movement of the body. These two are provided for by distinct lines or nerve fibres; and in all cases, these two sets are combined in a centre, thereby securing that the two sets be coöperative, unitedly contributing to the management of the living organism. This appears even if we take for illustration an organism so low as the *ascidian mollusk*, which floats in the water as if it were a sack drawn together towards the top, bulging out below; and which is nourished simply by the passing of a current of water in at the mouth, and out at a vent towards the lower end of the sac. A series of nerve lines comes from the mouth; a distinct ramification spreads over the lower portion of the sac; and these two are united in a single knot or ganglion, a little above the vent. By these contrivances, this little body, though for the most part stationary, is sensitive to the approach of any thing injurious, and by contraction of its mass expels the water with considerable force, driving the injurious matter to a distance. This combination of the two sets of nerves appears more strikingly in such an animal as the *centipede*, along whose body are successive groups of nerves, combined in regular order in a series of knots, and united longitudinally by connecting threads, attaching the successive knots. The same plan is carried up into a more articulated form in the case of the *winged insect*, with head, antennæ or feelers projecting from the head, wings, and legs, leading to a more marked appearance of separate combinations, giving greater prominence to the head. When from this we rise to the *fish*, thence to the *bird*, thence to the *quadruped*, we find the head made conspicuously the central organ of the entire nerve system of the animal, while it occupies the front position in the body. It is no longer one of a set or series of knots; nor even the largest or more conspicuous in a graduated order of centres; but in the head of the animal is found that which is the true nerve centre for the whole nerve system, designated the brain. In the case of the vertebrates, not only does the skeleton afford the solid frame-work on which the muscular system is built, but the back-bone contains within it the main column of nerve fibres, which are given out at the several joints according to the requirements of the body.

If meanwhile we concentrate attention on our own bodies, we may by the aid of personal experience find easy illustration of the prominent features of the nerve system. We shall take first the *two distinct lines* of nerves already mentioned, the one set concerned with sensibility, the other with movement of the muscles. From the tips of the fingers there run lines of nerve fibre, which are brought into combination at the wrist, and are carried up the arm, and onward by the shoulder and upper portion of the back-bone to the head. These are the nerves of *sensibility*, by means of which, as by telegraph wires, the slightest impression made on the tips of the fingers is instantly conveyed to the great nerve centre in the brain. Distinct from these is another set of nerves issuing from the brain, and descending the arm, giving off its fibres as it passes to the several muscles above the elbow, next to those above the wrist, and next to the muscles of the hand and fingers. These are the nerves of *movement*, by means of which the whole arm may be brought into action at pleasure, or the hand may be set to work, while the arm is at rest.

These two sets of nerves—the sensory and motor—are exactly *similar in structure*, consisting of an outer covering, within which floating in a white fluid is a thread which constitutes the nerve proper. The outer covering provides for *isolation* of the fibre, from other fibres laid alongside of it, just as copper wire is isolated by a gutta-percha covering when the two connecting lines from an electric battery are laid down in close proximity as in the arrangement for electric bells. By this provision the nerve fibres are completely isolated making it possible to distinguish sensory impressions so as to tell which finger has been touched. The similarity of structure in the two lines of nerves is a striking fact in view of the completely distinct functions fulfilled. This leads to a special explanation of the provision for different modes of action. This is secured by *diversity in the terminal arrangements* for the two classes of nerves. The nerves of sensibility have a peculiarly sensitive arrangement spread under the skin, constituting an end-bulb or touch organ. In certain parts of the body more sensitive than others, such as the tips of the fingers, there are additional minute corpuscles, grouped alongside of the nerve, liable to contract under the slightest pressure, and which add greatly to the sensitiveness of the particular parts about which they cluster. The terminal arrangements of the motor nerves are quite different. The nerve fibres pass into the substance of the muscle to be moved by them, and the nerve fibre is subdivided and distributed, so as to bring the several parts of the muscle under control. These fibres are so laid and connected, that a whole set of muscles can be moved simultaneously, being made to work in perfect harmony.

The vital activity of this whole arrangement of nerve fibres, including sensory and motor in one system, depends upon living connection of all with the great nerve centre in the brain, where the nerve energy is provided which keeps all in functional activity. Only, there is this striking difference with the two sets of fibres, that in the case of the sensory nerve the pulsation of energy is upwards to the brain, in the case of the motor nerve it is downwards towards the muscle. There is no scientific explanation yet reached of this contrast of molecular action. But by means of it the one order of nerves plays the part of a vehicle of impression providing for knowledge of what is without, the other order fulfils the part of an instrument for moving the muscular system which is part of the organism itself.

These two orders are not, however, to be

regarded as separate systems quite apart from each other, but as two sides of one system, which are essentially and closely related to each other. There is a provision for *combined action* of the two sets, so that an impulse communicated along a sensory nerve or set of nerves, may pass over to the motor system and terminate in muscular activity. This is most simply illustrated by the circumstance that the nerves of sensibility become instruments of *pain*, when a severe shock or blow is given, or some injury is inflicted. Suffering becomes a signal of risk and instantly the injured part shrinks or starts away from the source of suffering. This is a phase of sensori-motor activity illustrating a law which has a wide range of application in animal life. This sketch of the arrangements and functions of the two sides of the nerve system though traced in view of its application to human nature, will suffice to indicate the general plan in accordance with which sensibility and muscular activity are provided for in the animal kingdom generally. The ramification of the nerve lines will in each case be according to the simplicity or complexity of structure belonging to the animal; but the provisions for sensitiveness to touch, and power of movement are in all cases the same. Fish, bird, and quadruped are alike sensitive to touch, and they are alike capable of movement, though the mechanical contrivances by which locomotion is secured vary greatly; but a double distribution of nerve fibres in all cases provides for these two characteristics of animal life.

From this, we advance to the nerve centre,—the brain,—to which the nerves of sensibility run up, and from which the nerves of motion come forth. Here also there is identity in the nature of the organ, while there is variety in its size, with more or less complicated plans of arrangement, according to the extent of the nerve system of which it is the central organ. Still keeping to the human body for illustration, we may find in the most complex organism known to us illustration of what holds good in the main so far as essential structure is concerned.

The brain is made up of two entirely distinct substances. In the interior of the organ, and altogether concealed from view when a drawing of it is made, or the organ itself is exposed to observation, is *a white mass* consisting of a multitude of fibres. These are simply crowds of nerve lines gathered together, led up from the extremities and trunk, or provided for intercommunication with the several parts of this central organ. Gathered all round about this, and constituting the external mass, on the summit, sides, and base of the brain, is a completely distinct substance known as *the grey matter*, folded up in wavings, twistings, or convolutions, enclosing myriads of cells from which nerve energy is discharged. These cells differ considerably in form and size, suggesting the possibility of distinct functions being assigned to cells of different structure, some being smaller and less intimately connected with those around, others so much larger and more important as to have suggested the name of pyramidal cells, and also having lines of connection between themselves and other parts much more numerous than in the case of the smaller cells. Every cell has a nucleus or central point, which is the centre of vitality, while the fibres which they send out, varying in number from one to four or five, establish connection between cells, or pass into the nerves proper. These cells are packed together in a soft glutinous substance, in the outer layer of which they are fewer in number; approaching the interior, they become more numerous; and they are both more abundant, larger in size, and more distinguished by the number of their protoplasmic * fibres as they lie nearer to the mass of nerve fibres. In this crowd of nerve cells are the stores of nerve energy supplied to the nerve system, with every exercise of which molecular changes in the brain are believed to take place. On this account there must be regular and ample supply of nourishment for the brain, for which such provision has been made that, according to Haller's computation, one fifth part of the whole blood supply goes to the brain.

Regarded as the great central organ, the brain is divided into two halves or hemispheres, from each one of which goes forth supply of nerve fibres and nerve energy for the opposite side of the body. Its greatest depth is in the central part, the front and back being rounded down, the frontal region being, however, considerably more massive than the rear. Besides this great central body, there are several dependent subordinate bodies

* Protoplasm, see Appendix VII.

placed underneath, and directly above the upper part of the spine. Most important of these is the *cerebellum*, or little brain, whose functions are now generally believed to be closely connected with the equilibrium of the body when moving. Somewhat nearer the centre, and quite under the brain proper is the *pons* or bridge, providing for the interlacing of the fibres on their way out from the the central organ, and just below that are certain elongated bodies (*medulla oblongata*), consisting of masses of fibre just above the spinal cord.

Before closing this very brief and hasty description of the nerve system, there is one peculiarly striking arrangement to which special reference may be made. The mass of nerve fibre which passes down within the back-bone constituting the spinal column, which is formed in two divisions equivalent to the hemispheres of the brain, gives out at each of the vertebræ or spinal joints a supply of nerve for the portion of the body contiguous. This supply is sent out from each side of the column, and issues in two roots, a posterior and anterior; the posterior root being a body of sensory nerves, the anterior root of motor nerves. Shortly after passing out, these two form into one, uniting to constitute a nerve trunk. Just after they have thus united, the trunk again opens up into two, and in each one of these two a share of the sensory and motor roots finds a place, and thus preparation is made for sending out towards both the front and back of the body suitable proportion of both sets of nerves. The two roots drawn together as if to bind them into one, are by some inexplicable process subdivided, and the two bands issuing from the united band are found to have each a share of the contents of each root. Of all the singular occurrences coming under scientific observation there is nothing more surprising. The fact is certain, but there is no scientific explanation of the contrivance by which such a singular result is secured.

Having now before us in outline a representation of the nervous system of man, and having in this a guide to the understanding of the prominent features involved in the distribution of two orders of nerves over the body, and their concentration in a central organ, we are prepared for considering the comparative brain development presented to view as we ascend the scale of animal life. The main features of gradation may be shortly stated. In all cases, the brain is a soft pulpy body, composed as described, the exterior portion being cellular tissue, the interior fibrous, from the gathering of nerve lines. In the lowest orders of animals, the brain is of very small size. In the *insects*, such as the ant, bee, and wasp, it is only a slight band stretching from eye to eye. In the whole order of *fishes* an advance in organization appears, though the brain is small relatively to the size of the body, a fact which seems readily explained by the fact that there is little articulation in the structure of the fish, the whole body moving in one mass, by simple management of the fins and tail. The brain as a rule is simply two small round lobes of smooth surface laid together; and what is most to be remarked is that the brain proper is quite inferior in size to lobes of vision.* In front of the brain are slight strands connected with the organ of smell; and behind it are the two large lobes known as optic lobes, before which

* Unless references are otherwise given, illustration of the structure of brain here referred to, will be found in my work, *The Relations of Mind and Brain*, from p. 125, onwards.

the brain appears comparatively insignificant. This is the ordinary arrangement, but in the case of the shark the brain extends to much larger proportions, greatly surpassing the optic lobes, and having in front of it unusually ample provision for the organ of smell.*

When we reach the *reptiles* the normal order appears which continues thereafter up the whole range of animal life. The brain takes precedence of the lobes of special sense, and is the most important organ. This appears quite decisively in the brain of the frog. On account of the possession of four limbs, and its power of locomotion by forward leaps, provided for by the superior size and strength of the hind legs, there is much greater need for distribution of nerve lines, to place distinct muscles under control, and as a consequence the brain or central organ assumes a position of greater importance.

Passing next to *birds*, we find a marked advance in the structure of the brain. The two hemispheres are considerably extended towards the rear, and the two optic lobes underneath the back part of the brain are separated from each other, being placed some-

* *The Brain as the Organ of Mind*, by Dr. Bastian, p. 115.

what to the side. The cerebellum, or little brain, regulating equilibrium becomes more important in size and form, being laid up in transverse furrows. These important advances indicate a life of much more varied activity than in the lower orders. This animal walks, hops, perches on branches by the clutching of its claws, and flies from place to place. To provide for these varied forms of activity, there must be a more detailed arrangement of nerve system, which is clearly indicated in the complexity of the central organ.

The next advance introduces to notice the *smaller quadrupeds*, known as the rodents, of which the rat, rabbit, and hare may be taken as the most familiar examples. Here we still have the smooth surface of the brain, without any subdivision and twining into folds such as afterwards appears, but it is somewhat elongated in shape. An additional element here comes into view, that is, extra provision for acuteness of smell, in accordance with the well-known characteristics of the class of animals. Set out in front of the brain are two distinct lobes, which are the olfactory lobes. Wherever these are so placed in front of the brain, it is a clear proof that the life of the animal is largely directed by smell, that is, in a relatively greater degree than by sight, though constantly using the organs of vision with rapidity and acuteness. The cerebellum is in all cases prominent to the rear, presenting the laminated appearance always distinctive of the organ.

We now make a very marked transition in the development of brain, introducing to view the doubled or convoluted form occasioned by the folding of the material in a series of windings,—a form which is in complete contrast from the smooth surface characteristic of the brain in all lower orders. This series of windings or convolutions appears quite decidedly in the brain of the *cat*, in a manner very similar in the brain of the *dog*, and with still greater beauty and amplitude of fold in the brain of the *horse*. This folding process which is resorted to in the case of all the higher quadrupeds, seems a contrivance by which it is possible to pack a greater amount of material in such a way as to expose a greater degree of surface, within the narrow space at command inside the cranium. In all the three examples named, great prominence is given to the bulbs of smell, which are spread out quite conspicuously in front of the brain,—implying, as in lower examples, a life largely governed by sense of smell.

Omitting special reference to animals of great bulk, and possessing enormous muscular power, such as the elephant and the whale, both of which have singularly complicated and beautiful brains, I pass to the races of *monkeys* and *apes*, which are nearest in structure to man. In these animals the configuration of body is certainly the nearest approach to the human figure which is to be found anywhere in the animal kingdom. They can not, indeed, assume the perfectly erect posture of man, but they come very near to it; and though they move on all four limbs, feeling themselves more secure in that mode of advance, they have a formation of hand analogous to that of man, with a distinctly formed thumb, enabling them to grasp an object in a manner closely resembling the human grasp. The apes have even an advantage over the human race, for they have a thumb on the foot, as well as on the hand; which may also have its own disadvantages, for it might prove no convenience to us if we were so endowed.

But the presence of the thumb on the lower extremities suggests the use which it serves in the animal's ordinary life, in grasping the branches along which it moves. If from the similarity of outward configuration, we pass to contemplate the brain, we find here also great similarity of structure. And indeed if the relations of muscle, nerve, and brain be as already indicated, it follows from the resemblances of outward form that there must be a greater resemblance between the brain of man and the brain of the monkey and of the ape, than between the human brain and that of any other animal known to us. And so it proves to be. The brain of the monkey has its subdivisions and convolutions very similar to those of the human brain, only the convolutions are simpler in arrangement. In outline it is deficient only in the diminished bulk of the front part, and also the back part of the organ; but in its expansion it resembles the human brain in this, that to the rear it spreads back over the cerebellum, so as to cover it. The brain of the ape, including under this designation the orang, gorilla, and chimpanzee, is in still closer resemblance to the human, being still, however, somewhat simpler in the arrangement of its convolutions, but so closely approximating that the exact state of the case is as nearly as possible described, if we say that the brain of the ape, while it is decidedly smaller, appears like a miniature of the human brain in a slightly undeveloped state.*

The human brain is an elaborate organ, exceedingly complicated in its convolutions. We can not, indeed, describe it as the most convoluted, for the brain of the elephant is at least as distinguished for the beauty and complication of its folding, and the brain of the whale is far more minute and detailed, presenting quite a multitude of minute convolutions. For descriptive purposes, the human brain is divided into four superficial areas, known as lobes, and pretty clearly defined by certain natural boundaries. From the lower part of the organ, entering at a point scarcely half way back is a fissure or cutting running up into the mass in a direction uniformly inclining towards the rear, known as the Sylvian fissure; while coming over the summit, at a point near the middle, and inclining down towards that just described, is another fissure, known as the fissure of Rolando. By these

* See Appendix XI.

two deeply cut hollows, the brain is marked off into four separate areas superficially, a front and a rear lobe; and two central lobes, the one upper and the other under. Besides this there is a concealed and isolated lobe, described on account of its situation as an island, which is covered from view by the overlapping of the two sides of the Sylvian fissure. Such is a description in outline of the configuration of the human brain, to which must be added the statement that each lobe is filled in with its own special arrangement of convolutions, each one having at least three well defined lines of convolution. Each of the hemispheres is similarly arranged, though not by any means quite identical in disposal of convolutions, yet the general description now given is strictly applicable to both. The two hemispheres, connected mainly with the ramification of nerve fibre running to the opposite sides of the body, are united together a considerable way down by a transverse band of nerve fibres, which at once unite the two into one organ, and make the union so effected a living efficient union by carrying a multitude of lines of communication from the one side to the other. Just below this, in the interior of the organ are two great central bodies, known as the basal ganglia, and consisting of nerve fibres massed together with grey matter around them, that in front being chiefly motor nerves brought to a junction, the latter sensory nerves combined in like manner. The same arrangement holds in both hemispheres, thereby providing that the respective masses of motor, and of sensory nerves lie exactly opposite each other. Behind these in the centre, lying in a position under both hemispheres are four small bulbs connected with the nerves of vision, and also with the cerebellum; and behind them, covered by the posterior lobe of the brain is the cerebellum itself, or little brain, largely concerned with coördination of movements, or equilibrium of the two sides of the system. Just below these arrangements the two great cords of nerve fibre descend towards the body, which are covered by a transverse mass, known as the bridge, appearing complete as a crossing, and containing transverse fibres from the cerebellum, as well as a series of longitudinal fibres. Immediately underneath the bridge are pillars or masses of nerve, constituting the crowning portion of the spinal system, and formed in eight distinct bodies, the two in front and the two in rear being elongated and known as pyramids, those in the centre being rounded in figure. From the elongated bodies, the nerve fibres pass across to the opposite sides of the body. This gathering is known as the *medulla oblongata.* Just beneath comes the spinal canal, from which at the different joints of the spine are given out a suitable supply of sensory and motor nerves as previously described.

Having thus given a general account of the central arrangements of the nerve system of the human body, it is important to state that an order of things closely analogous obtains in other and lower orders of organism, in respect of interior plan, so that if the interior of the brain of the dog were laid open to view it would present a plan of distribution very similar to that now described.

To complete the view of the functions of the brain as indicated by recent research, I have next to give a brief account of an extended course of experiments of great delicacy designed to ascertain whether it may be possible to localize certain functions within a definite area of the brain. All are familiar with the fanciful subdivisions of the outer surface of the human skull, under the name of phrenology, represented on moulds of the head, all marked with dividing lines and figures. This pretentious and unscientific assumption of knowledge which no one possessed, has had its time of popularity, aided by a general recognition of comparative superiority in head formation in persons of known ability. Any thing equivalent to an exact partition of the bony covering protecting the brain, has not been favored by scientific observations; but these fanciful maps of the head, which have been sold cheap, and fully certified, may serve as a guide to a general notion of what has been attempted on the surface of the brain itself, after removal of the skull. The illustrative aid, however, consists in nothing more than the suggestion of distinct areas, for there is no analogy between what has been discovered by the observations now to be described, and the "bumps" alleged to be found on the cranium.

The conjecture which may be said to have originated experiments as to localization was that there was a close resemblance between the action of nerve energy, and an electric current. The attempt made was to similate the action of the nerve cells, by discharging a current of electricity upon the grey matter of the brain, and recording the results which came under observation. Experiments were begun in 1870 in Germany by Fritsch and Hitzig, the dog being the animal experimented upon. The investigation was undertaken also by Dr. Ferrier of King's College London, and much more extended and varied results were published by him in 1873. Confirmatory work, executed with many precautions, was undertaken on the subject in 1874 by a committee of the New York Society of Neurology and Electrology,—a committee which included Drs. Dalton, Arnold, Beard, Flint, and Masson,—testing results by frequent renewal of the experiments; and at the same time, a similar course of inquiry was being conducted in Paris by Carville and Duret.*

By these investigations, the possibility of electric stimulation of the cortical or grey matter of the brain, and consequent activity of the nerve system has been fully established; and though there is still considerable diversity

* For detailed narrative, see my work on *The Relations of Mind and Brain*, chap. iv. p. 79.

of opinion concerning the interpretation of the facts, it can not be disputed that by directing the electrode on certain well defined areas of the surface of the brain, it is possible to bring into natural activity certain portions of the muscular system, as controlled by the motor nerves.

The plan adopted is, after putting the animal into an insensible state by use of chloroform, and removing the cranium so as to expose the brain, to apply the electrode connected with an electric battery to a given point on the surface, record the result, and gradually shift the needle round the original spot until a new result is obtained, in which the spot previously tested becomes an index for the boundary of one circle, and this marks the fact that a new circle has been entered.

By this process of investigation a series of centres for active stimulation have been discovered. These number, in the brain of the rat, six; in the brain of the rabbit, seven; of the cat, eleven; of the dog, thirteen; and of the monkey, at least, seventeen. A curious limitation to the area of experiment has been encountered here, for all the centres identified are found to cluster over the central region of the brain, and both the front and rear parts of the organ are silent, offering no response however greatly stimulated. The explanation of this silence remains a matter of doubt. It may be that these portions of the brain are concerned with movements which do not come under the observation of the operator, or that they are centres of sensibility from which no movement can naturally follow, or that they fulfil functions which can not be recognized by this mode of experiment. Uncertainty hangs over this department in the investigation.

The actual results may be indicated by a few examples. At a point well forward in the brain of the dog, marked number one by Ferrier, is a centre which when stimulated leads to movement of the hind leg on the opposite side; and by exciting another portion of the brain quite contiguous, marked number four, movement of the opposite fore leg is produced. By exciting a point situated over these two and on a distinct convolution, wagging of the tail is induced. By transferring the needle to a point much lower down, towards the base of the brain, but still well forward, marked by Ferrier nine, the mouth is opened and the tongue moved, while in many cases a decided bark is emitted. These examples may suffice to indicate the class of results obtained; and similar results have been seen in all animals subjected to this test, with such variations as may be considered inevitable in view of the configuration of the animal.

While distinct areas or circles of the brain have thus been marked, warranting localizing of certain functions, the facts connected with these experiments do not favor the view that each area is to be taken as so rigidly distinct that it may be supposed to operate separately in a quite isolated manner. On the contrary, a conjoint action of several centres seems more commonly implied when the natural activity of the brain is contemplated in line of these results. Additional weight must be given to this consideration, when it is noticed that the centres are nominally *motor centres*,—movement and not sensibility being the result most patent to the observer,—nevertheless on closer scrutiny it proves true, that many of the movements occasioned by electric stimulation are those induced naturally as the result of sensation. Such for example are the movements of the eyelids consequent upon a dazzling of the eyes, or movement of the ears because of a startling sound. In this way it becomes clear that within a given area a centre of sensibility is in communication with a motor centre close by, or it may be even at some little distance. Thus this most delicate and difficult course of investigation supports the view that much of the activity of the animal organism is provided for by an established connection between nerve cells respectively presenting the terminus in the brain for a sensory nerve, and the starting point for a motor nerve, or point of communication with such a nerve. From this conclusion, it follows that a very large amount of the activity which we witness in the case of animals, often attributed to instinct, or even to voluntary determination, is to be described as *sensori-motor activity*. That is to say, the action is brought about by a contrivance which may be described as partly mechanical, partly chemical. Its history may be sketched in this way: an impression is made on one of the nerves of sensibility, or on one of the organs of special sense, such as the eye or ear; a wave of impulse passes along the incarrying nerve fibre, leading to molecular change in the nerve cell, and to sensibility in some way unknown; the excitation occasioned there is extended along a connecting fibre to a second nerve cell, which is the starting point for a motor nerve; along that line the impulse is instantly and inevitably continued; and as an almost instantaneous result, without any form of sensibility to indicate what is taking place, the muscular energy is liberated, and action is the direct consequence. The problem which immediately arises is this,—How far may the activity of all living organism be accounted for in this way, including even the activity of man? This is a problem which will present an interesting subject for discussion in the next stage of this inquiry, the import of which must now be made apparent by the sketch of the structure of the nerve system, and the results of the experiments as to localization.

Nothing more is now required to complete this narrative leading up to this problem, and discovering its proportions, than a brief account of correlative inquiry which has afforded strong confirmatory evidence as to the truth of the conclusions favoring localization, and coördinate action of different portions of the brain as the central organ governing the whole nerve system. The corroberative evidence at once supporting the conclusions as to localization and favoring their extension to human nature is obtained by reference to the results of injury to the nerve system at various parts of the body, and injury to the brain as ascertained after death. Continuing experiments on the animals, it has been shown that even if a portion of the brain be cut away, it is still possible to operate on the nerve lines in the usual manner by means of electricity. Pushing experiment in this direction still further it has been found that more serious injury permanently destroys the centre, and entails paralysis of the muscles controlled by it when in a healthy state. In like manner it has been proved that if the nerve itself be cut, the communication is at an end, and movement by stimulation has become impossible.

By perpetually occurring cases of paralysis in human experience, and careful examination after death of the exact situation and extent of disease in the brain, it has been shown by accumulation of evidence, that the laws which provide for sensibility and for muscular activity in the history of the lower animals, do also hold in the case of man. While the brain continues in full vigor, all the usual forms of sensibility, and modes of action are simple; where these have become disturbed, restricted or impossible, some injury has been accidentally inflicted on the brain of the sufferer, or disease has begun in the organ, and has gained a hold exactly proportionate to the forms of restraint and disturbance which have become outwardly manifest. These are results which show how much is due by way of sympathy, and patience, and encouragement to those who suffer under any degree of brain injury or disease, due from all around them whose conduct may have any part in determining their experience. These results testify how closely the human organism stands allied to lower orders of organism around; how many homologies of structure there are, and how many analogies in experience. These things declare that science has a clear and unchallangeable field of inquiry in seeking an explanation of human nature on the same lines of procedure as those which have been followed in ascending the scale of living organism. The nature and extent of materials at its disposal as the result of the most recent investigations have now been indicated. The problem is, How far can the anatomy and physiology of the human frame account for the facts of human life? The strength and practical power of religious thought in the world will depend upon the answer, for science must here carry some test of religion. On the other hand, the problem which human life presents is by far the most severe test which science has to encounter. In facing the facts, science is engaged with the settlement of its own boundaries,—the demonstration of its own limits. In facing this highest problem which human observation encounters,—man's explanation of himself,—let us cease from comparisons between scientific claims and religious, and let us face with patience and resolution the question—What is the exact place, and what the destiny of man, who has piled up the sciences, and midst the turmoil and conflict of life, has found his most elevating exercise, and most profound calm, in worship of "the King eternal, immortal, invisible, the only wise God"?

LECTURE VI. No. 1.

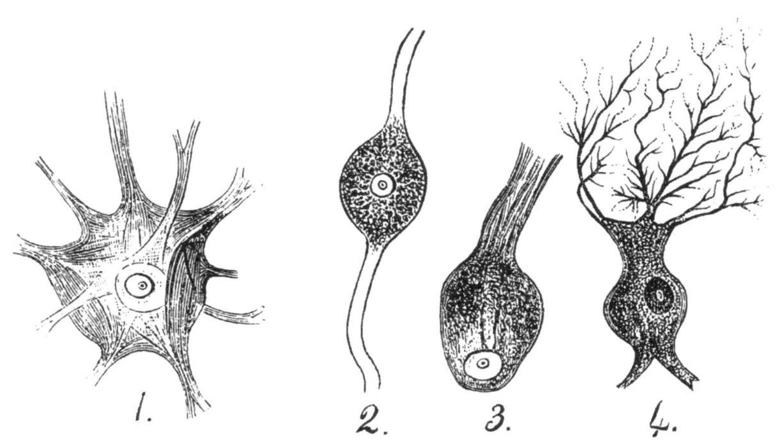

NERVE CELLS.

1. MULTIPOLAR. 2. BIPOLAR. 3. UNIPOLAR. 4. CELL WITH RAMIFICATION. NUCLEUS OR LIFE CENTRE IS MARKED IN EACH.

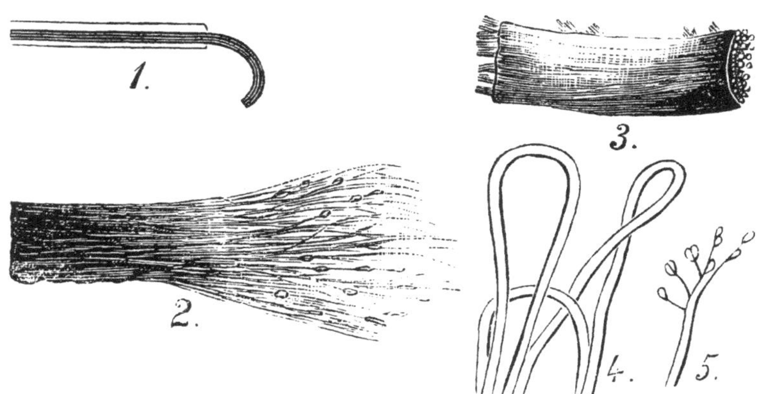

NERVE FIBRES.

1. SECTION, SHOWING NERVE SHEATH CUT, AND NERVE LINE PROJECTING. 2. BUNDLE OF NERVES SPLIT UP INTO FILAMENTS. 3. COMBINATION OF NERVES. 4. NERVE LOOPS. 5. SENSORY CORPUSCLES ON THE NERVE FIBRES.

LECTURE VI. No. 2.

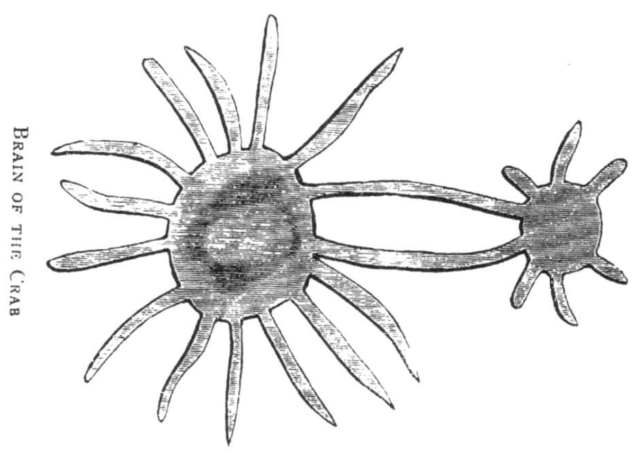

Brain of the Crab

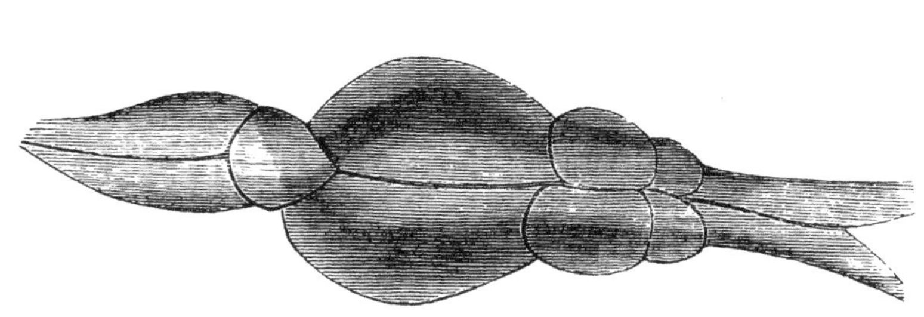

Brain of the Cod,
the two larger lobes being those of vision, the brain
being in front of these.

LECTURE VI. No. 3.

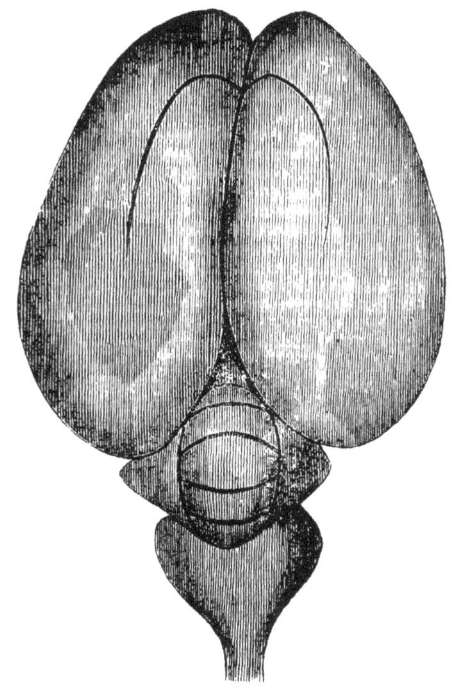

BRAIN OF THE BIRD.

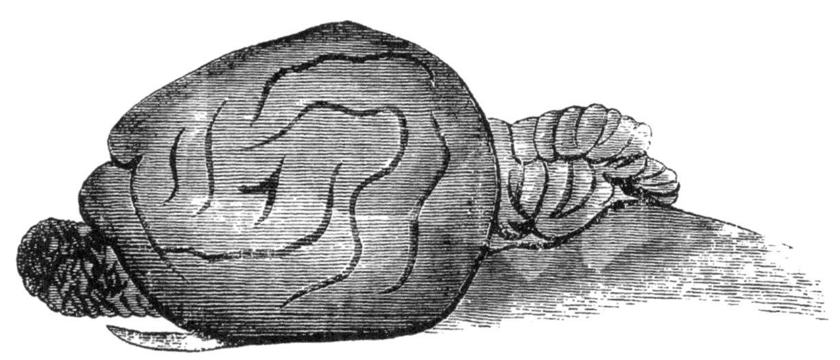

BRAIN OF THE CAT,
WITH BULB OF SMELL IN FRONT, AND LITTLE BRAIN BEHIND.

LECTURE VI. No. 4.

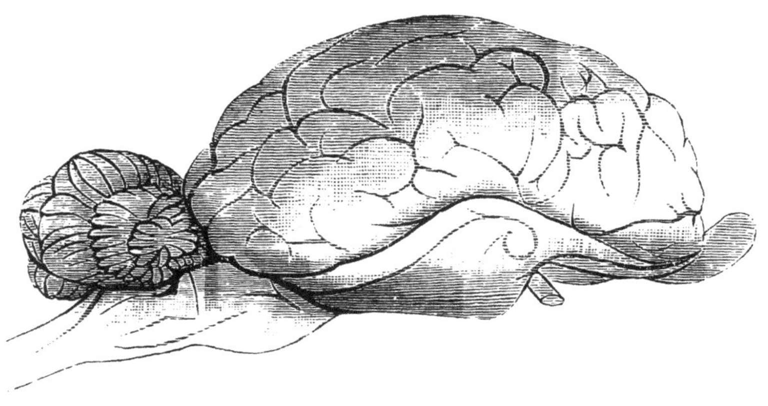

Brain of Horse,
WITH BULB OF SMELL IN FRONT, LITTLE BRAIN IN REAR.

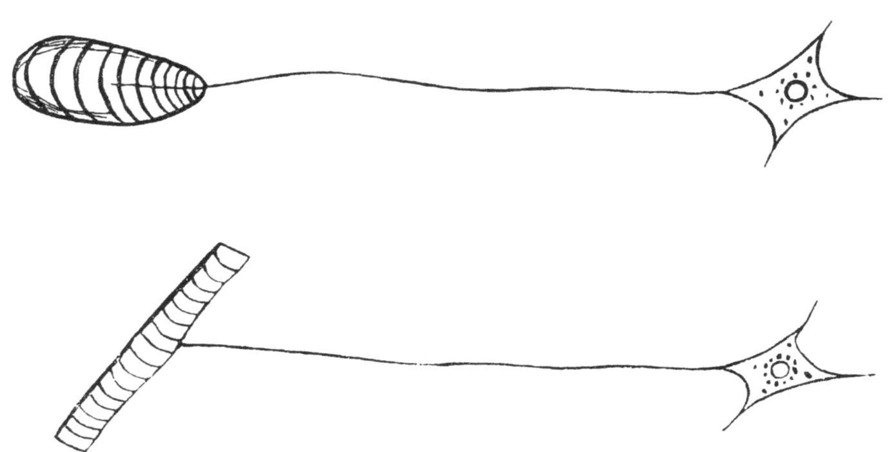

Diagram of Sensory and Motor Apparatus.
THE UPPER IS THE SENSORY, WITH BULB, NERVE LINE, AND NERVE CELL.
THE UNDER IS THE MOTOR, WITH MUSCLE, NERVE LINE, AND NERVE CELL.

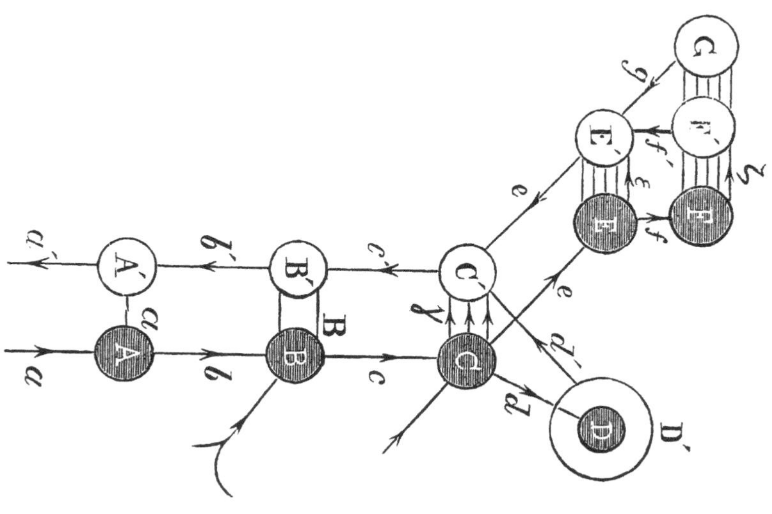

DIAGRAM OF CEREBRO-SPINAL NERVE CENTRES.
DARK REPRESENTING SENSORY; THE LIGHT, MOTOR CENTRES. THE ARROWS INDICATE THE DIRECTION OF THE CURRENT OF INFLUENCE.

NERVE SYSTEM OF THE INSECT, SHOWING DISTINCT CENTRES.

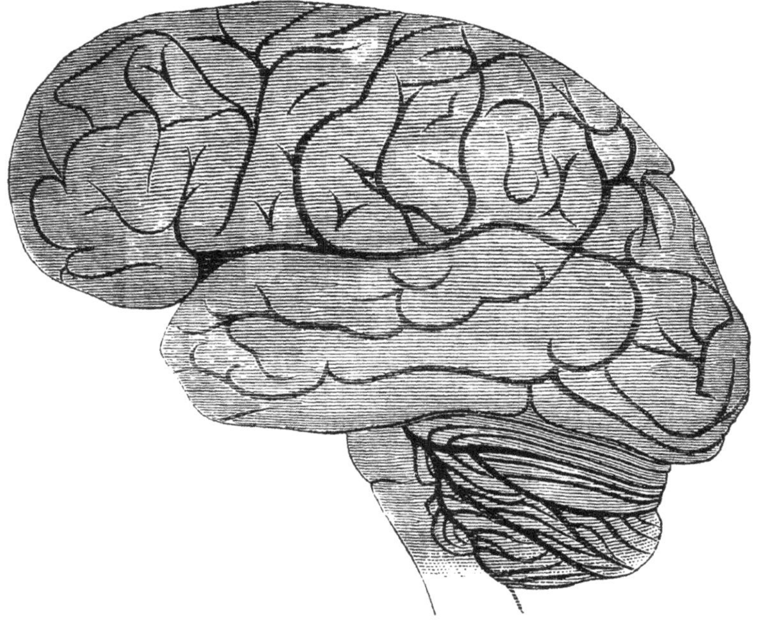

HUMAN BRAIN.

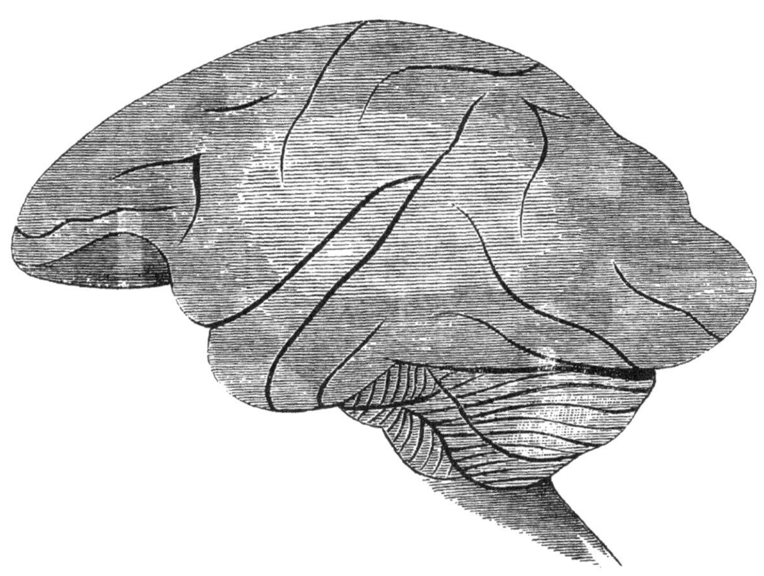

BRAIN OF MONKEY,

LECTURE VI. No. 7.

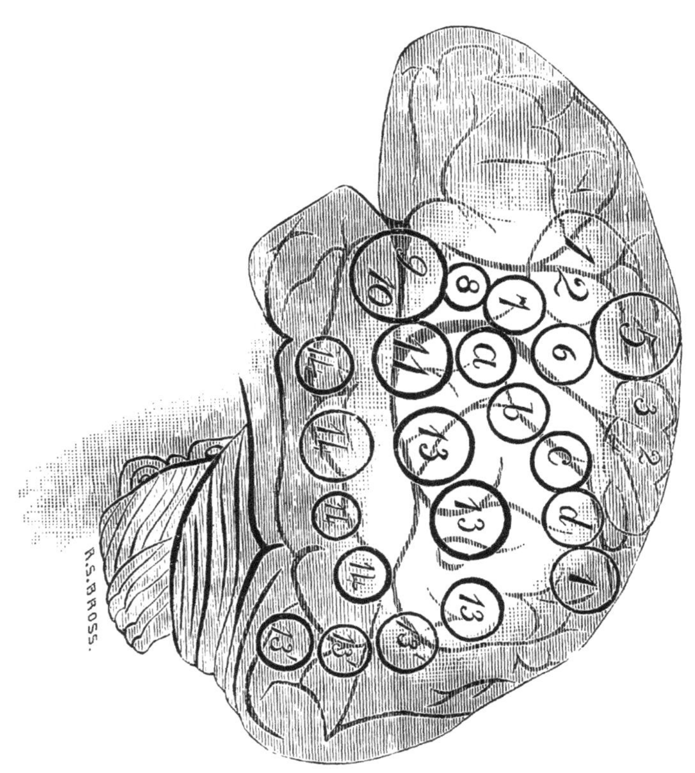

HUMAN BRAIN,
WITH CENTRES OF ELECTRIC EXCITATION.

LECTURE VII.

MAN'S PLACE IN THE WORLD.

THE accumulated interest gathered around the direct and collateral investigations bearing on the development of species, has naturally turned greatly increased attention on man's position in the universe. As has been shown by study of the nervous system belonging to animal life, all organism has been constructed on a uniform plan, advancing in complication as the organism becomes more intricate in structure, having separate parts assigned to distinct functions. This uniform plan is seen to culminate in man. Thus it follows, that man appears to the scientific observer, as the last or most advanced figure in a gradually ascending scale. That this is man's place in the field of organized existence no one will doubt.

The prevailing view of our nature, however, recognizes more in it than bone, muscle, nerve, and cellular tissue, while observational science is capable of recognizing no more than these, so that, if there be any thing more, it is quite beyond the range of physical science, and within the territory of mental philosophy. Here then, is preparation for conflict, which may be accepted as inevitable, because of the advance of science. The occasion for this expectation should, however, be fully understood. Its certainty may be maintained on two obvious grounds. The first is concerned with the history of scientific progress. Science is pushing its way up the extended scale of existence with no exact knowledge of its own limits; knowing what its achievements have been, animated to a high degree by the vastness of the problems still before it, but knowing nothing quite definite as to its own boundaries. The aggressive force of science at such a stage must be great. On the other hand, there is a large body of settled conviction, which has swayed men and moulded society in all ages, which is an opposing force operating on that very line along which science is advancing, and which must be encountered whenever man's place in the universe becomes the subject of inquiry. This opposing conviction is not necessarily religious in type, though it is supported by the whole range of thought concerned with the supernatural. The conviction here referred to, as lying more obviously across the path on which science is travelling, is that concerned with the personality of man, with the rights and responsibilities of individuals, implying accepted conclusions on which the government, and police, and administration of affairs in every nation are based. It must, then, be clearly recognized that the conflict anticipated as inevitable is the conflict of knowledge of one order, with knowledge of a different order. It is conflict of knowledge obtained by the slow and difficult processes available to science, with knowledge possessed by all, applied in the regulation of individual and social life, and systematized in the annals of mental philosophy; or, we may more nearly describe the condition of matters by saying that the occasion of conflict is the determination of science to include all within its own area, rather than the possession of actual knowledge as to the highest order of life, for science is only seeking, and can not profess to have found, an explanation of the functions of human life, as it can profess to have done in the case of lower orders. There could, therefore, be no more mistaken representation of the pending conflict than the allegation that it is a conflict of knowledge with ignorance. To put it in the best light for science, it is the conflict of one kind of knowledge with another; but there is a nearer approach to accuracy if we say that the conflict is occasioned by the *want of verified conclusions* within the boundaries of science itself, in contrast with very definite conclusions belonging to men generally, and verified by practical tests which scientific men can not refuse. It is not essential to the point, but may be of consequence in view of the range of application belonging to this inquiry, to remark that religious thought is not itself directly involved here; nevertheless, religious thought is deeply concerned in the issue of the conflict.

Having thus briefly indicated the occasion of the conflict, and the contending forces, it is desirable to find the standpoint of science. The nature and origin of life having been passed as problems for which no solution has yet been found, science has concentrated on the functions of the various portions of each organism, and on the contrivances for its protection and continuance in the world; and still more in advance, on the laws favoring the development of species. From outward form it has passed to inward structure, and pressing still more closely towards the secrets of life has endeavored to ascertain by microscopic investigation what provision has been made for maintaining the vital processes involved in the action of organism. Travelling up the advancing orders of animate existence, science has discovered a uniform plan adapted to varying complexity of structure. Thus entered and far advanced on the course of investigation, science sees no limit to its field of inquiry save the limits of organism itself. What has already been achieved, gives full warrant for the claim of inclusion, in which all scientific men naturally concur, and with which men generally will readily agree. This agreement, however, lies on the very boundary line of disagreement and dissension. Immediately when an attempt is made to set forth what is implied, it becomes clear that some scientific men include very large expectations as to what science is yet to accomplish; while others, showing more of the caution of the scientific spirit, decline to commit themselves to dogmatic assertions. Up to the line of agreement indicated we are dealing with science; beyond that line, where we come upon disagreements, we are not dealing with science, but with the comparative sanguineness or caution of scientific men.

What we have before us as clearly admitted on all sides is that human life presents the common characteristics of organic life, and is subjected to the ordinary laws of organism. The problem with which we have now to deal in view of this admission is this, —How far do the functions of organism account for the universally recognized characteristics of human life?

In facing this problem there are not a few scientific inquirers who look upon the mere raising of it as a claim to include all that belongs to human nature within the realm of physical science. They have allowed themselves to regard the two things as interchangeable, and all their researches are in their view so involved in this identification, that they resent the challenging of it, as if it implied antagonism to science. But the scientific inconsistency of this is easily shown. That science must extend its investigations to human organism, admits of no doubt; that by means of this investigation all the phenomena of human life will be traced to organism, is the very thing to be proved, and until established on clear and full evidence is not to be regarded otherwise than problematic. If we are in this matter to be influenced by regard to the slow and difficult procedure in cases of much greater simplicity, we shall be guarded in the utterance of expectations; if we make account of the enormous difficulties to be encountered in arranging the facts to be explained, we shall be still more guarded; and if we remember that the practical demands of life must all be met day by day without waiting for science as an aid, it will not appear strange that the non-scientific thinker regards the whole scientific investigation as wide of the sphere in which questions of self-government are settled, even though this view seems to affirm, without knowledge of both sides, that there is a sphere belonging to human life into which science can not enter.

Still, it must be allowed that in the pathway of science nothing is to be foreclosed, and no area, whether large or small, is to be shut off on which the appliances of science can be brought to bear. Science can not exclude man from the range of investigation; can not on any warrant supplied by the conditions of its own procedure, draw a line within the circumference of nature, even though it may be constrained to allow that there are many things within nature of which it can offer no explanation.

That science has by recent research done much to explain phases of human activity previously unexplained, may be clearly shown. The modification of previously received opinion may be indicated thus,—that many forms formerly regarded as in the true sense voluntary, and so described in the life not only of man, but also of the higher animals, can be explained by the action of brain and nerve. This involves a considerable extension of the area of the mechanical in human action, and a considerable restriction of the area of the voluntary. In seeking to indicate roughly the form of this restriction, we may find enough for our purpose in the distinction between what we may describe as *muscular action*, and what we would more naturally denominate *personal conduct*. This contrast will serve throughout, as we proceed to estimate the explanations which science has reached in dealing with the characteristics of human life.

The proved superiority of brain and nerve in man affords an adequate explanation of his generally recognized superiority in the variety of the forms of his muscular activity. In mere muscular power man can not compete with the more powerful animals. His practical superiority is seen in manipulation and the vastly greater variety of occupations to which he can turn; and in the greater wisdom he has for self-government. Leaving meanwhile out of account comparative intelligence, we have only to consider the superior use man has of the general sensibilities of the body, and of the special senses of touch and sight; the greater variety of the joints and muscles in his body; the more complicated arrangements of his nerve system; and the relation of all these in a single economy, in order to perceive a distinct phase of the superiority of man, sufficiently accounted for by clearly recognized facts, anatomical and physiological. In a multitude of well-known forms of action, of which the mechanical arts afford illustration, man can do what can not be attempted by lower forms of organism.

Another step higher is taken by the advance of physiological science, involving an explanation of *acquired aptitudes*. The interaction of sensibility and motor activity has been shown to be great. A message conveyed along a sensory line is readily transferred to a motor line; the sense of touch becomes a natural guide to familiar forms of action; a form of sensibility may thus be connected with a given range of motor apparatus, just as the history of the blind illustrates how much more can be accomplished by aid of touch without sight, than is ordinarily achieved. By these means, what at first requires consideration and care (neither of which is accounted for by physiological explanations), comes at last to be done without deliberation, and with so much facility, that it does not seem to engage much attention. Physiological science thus accounts for a considerable amount of superior activity characteristic of man in his daily engagements.

It must, however, be noticed that the explanation is not a complete one, inasmuch as the action of the sensory and motor apparatus referred to, presupposes consideration and care, that is intellectual and voluntary guidance commensurate with the initial difficulties of attainment, in order that the nerve system may be brought to accomplish what becomes possible afterwards by mere mechanical and chemical contrivance within the living organism.

Having thus briefly indicated the advances in knowledge of the working of our own organism gained by recent research, and the explanation thus afforded of much of the superiority manifest in human life, we come upon the grand difficulty of science,—How to account for *intellectual superiority*. It is obvious that animals give proofs of intelligence as well as men; and that the human brain has a marked superiority in the frontal region, to which intelligence is commonly referred, as it certainly is superior also in the back part of the organ, to which intelligence is not so commonly referred. But the pressing difficulty is this, to show how nerve cells, confessedly concerned with the development of nerve energy, and the production of sensory and motor activity, can be further considered capable of performing the function of thought, covering the whole variety of mental occupations. Attention has been directed to the recognized diversities of nerve cells, which are unipolar, bipolar, and multipolar, on the hypothesis that these diversities may point to differences of function so great as to provide what is required. But there is a total failure of evidence to substantiate this hypothesis. The differences among the nerve cells of the brain are differences in size, and in the number of the lines of communication taking rise from them. In accordance with the plan of arrangement everywhere recognized, the number of protoplasmic lines originating from a cell gives an index to the points of contact it has in the surrounding tissue, and thus to the part it may perform in the work of coördination or interaction. A small cell with only a single line or fibre proceeding from it, must be regarded as a cell conveying nerve stimulus in only a single direction, and to only a single destination. A bipolar cell in accordance with the same rule of interpretation, is a cell having communication in two opposite directions, and thus may be capable of transmitting stimulus by the one channel or by the other, besides which it is possible, so far as structure is concerned, that such a cell may receive stimulus from one direction and send it forth in an opposite, thus proving a centre of intercommunication. On the same plan, a multipolar cell, being of greater size, and having from five to ten fibres proceeding from it, holds a more important place in the manifold ramifications of cellular tissue, sending out stimulus in an increased variety of courses according to the number of the lines pertaining to it, and proving thus an intermediate station in communication with a variety of distinct centres. No observation yet directed upon the nerve cells has proved sufficient to establish all this, but the supposition is in strict harmony with what has been ascertained as to the laws governing the action of the nerve system.

When, however, an attempt is made to proceed farther, selecting the largest cells as "mind cells,"* or cells generating thought and volition, there is a complete break away

* Hæckel's *Evolution of Man*, vol. i. p. 129.

from evidence, and from the clear lines of interpretation already established. We are dealing with conjecture, not with science. There is no reason in the interests of truth to object to hypothesis in this region, any more than in another, for conjecture has often proved the handmaid of discovery, and it is likely to be so in a still larger degree. But an essential condition of this acknowledgment is, that conjecture do not claim any respect beyond what its nature warrants, and specially do not take to itself the name of science,—knowledge, or certainty. Beyond this, it must be recognized in every intelligent circle, that conjectures, like men of different character, are entitled to different degrees of respect, some to only a moderate and guarded measure, others to a very high degree, and some to very little indeed. In a case like the present, we can have no sure test for a provisional judgment entitled to regulate provisional procedure, other than the harmony of the conjecture with scientific knowledge already acquired as to the same region of existence. Judged by this test, the conjecture that the intellectual life of man is to be accounted for by the presence in the brain of myriads of thought cells, volitional cells, memory cells, imagination cells, and emotional cells, has little on which to claim a high degree of consideration. Its most obvious scientific difficulties are these two, that it implies a departure from the scheme of brain action scientifically established, and that it passes away from the scientific appliances employed to obtain knowledge of brain action. The real discoveries which have been made are the existence of sensory and motor apparatus, and the interaction of these two branches or divisions of the system. Beyond this, science has made no advance. The scientific appliances by which these discoveries have been reached are those available in post-mortem dissection, and in experiment under such exposure of the brain tissue as has been found compatible with functional activity of the organ. This conjecture of "mind-cells" does not either experimentally or logically connect itself with the recent advances in knowledge of the brain. The system of sensory and motor apparatus spread over the body for which the brain is the great central and governing organ does not under the scientific explanation of it already obtained, lead on by natural sequence to the conjecture of additional and greatly higher functions being assigned to the brain. Besides, the suggestion that place should be found in the brain for something more and higher than sensori-motor activity, does not come from any necessity which has arisen in the course of scientific observation. It is only because we know, in a manner quite different from that in which scientific knowledge of nerve and brain has been acquired, that man does observe, and reason, construct hypotheses and cherish expectations, contemplate rules of conduct and regulate his actions in accordance with them, that scientific inquirers, attempting to include the whole range of human powers, have felt themselves urged forward to seek an explanation of the characteristics of mental life which are the familiar facts of man's experience. The course of *experiment* has not brought them up to these facts; common acquaintance with them has pressed on scientific inquirers the need for dealing with them in order to make good the claim that science contains the explanation of all existence, man included. The dilemma for this conjecture that the brain thinks and wills is serious. If the brain is capable of what is commonly named *mental* activity, all that science has demonstrated is susceptibility and motor activity, that is nerve impulse involving molecular and muscular action, and this carries no explanation of mental action.

In this, as in previous cases, it is better to take purely scientific statements concerning the structure and functions of the nerve cells, without regard to theoretical result. The following quotations will show what account has been given of the variety of appearance and position of the nerve cells. Professor Turner says, nerve cells are "the characteristic structures in the nerve centres, are susceptible to impressions or nervous impulses, and are the texture in which the molecular changes occur that produce or disengage the special form of energy named nerve energy, the evolution of which is the distinctive mark of a nerve centre." * "The central extremities of the nerve fibres lie in relation to, and are often directly connected with the nerve cells." From opposite points of the surface of the *bi-*

* *Human Anatomy,* i. p. 198.

polar cell "a strong process is given off, which is directly continued into a nerve fibre.*" When we pass next to *multipolar cells*, we have the following explanations. "In many localities they present characteristic forms. In the gray matter of the *spinal cord*, more especially in its anterior horn,† they give rise to numerous processes, and have a stellate or radiate form. In the gray matter on the surface of the convolutions of the cerebrum they are pyramidal in shape; the apex is directed to the surface of the convolution, the base towards the white matter; the processes arise from the base, apex, and sides of the pyramid."‡ "The processes which arise from a multipolar nerve cell as a rule divide and subdivide as they pass away from the body of the cell, until at last they give rise to branches of extreme tenuity. These branching processes apparently consist exclusively of cell protoplasm, and have been called protoplasm processes. Gerlach has described the protoplasm processes of the multipolar nerve cells of the brain and spinal cord as forming an excessively minute net-work, from which mi-

* *Human Anatomy*, i. p. 199.

† From which motor nerves emerge. ‡ *Human Anat.*, i. p. 200.

nute medullated *nerve fibres* arise." * "From the observations of Lockhart Clark, Arndt, Cleland and Meynert, there can be no doubt that the pyramidal nerve cells vary in relative size and in numbers in the different layers of the gray cortex, and that the largest sized pyramidal cells lie in the third and fourth layers." † "Large pyramidal cells are found in the *frontal lobe* in considerable numbers," but it is added, "there is no difficulty in recognizing in the occipital lobe" (the back region of the brain) "a small proportion of cells quite equal in magnitude to the largest cells of the frontal lobe." ‡

From these statements, it is easy to judge what value can be attached to the conjecture that multipolar or pyramidal cells are to be regarded as "*mind-cells.*" The result may be summarized thus; (1) The larger cells are invariably distinguished by the number of fibres given off, or the lines of communication they have with other parts of the tissue; (2) As to distribution of these cell-fibres appearing in the brain, it is found that as the cells themselves are in the lower strata of the gray matter, the majority of their fibres stretch

* *Human Anat.*, i. p. 201. † *Ib.* p. 282. ‡ See Appendix XII.

downwards, the mass of the nerve fibres thus communicating with the organism; (3) These pyramidal cells are not peculiar to any part of the brain, and they do not belong to the brain alone, but are found in the gray matter of the spinal cord, and also of the sympathetic system, which provides for the action of the heart, lungs, and other vital organs. All these characteristics are adverse to the conjecture that for the larger sized cells a claim can be made assigning to them distinctively intellectual or mental functions.

In contrast with this view, I shall here introduce an extract from Hæckel's *Evolution of Man*, as he may be accounted the most advanced advocate of the theory of "mind-cells." He says,—"The nerve cell of the brain is an extremely one-sided formation. It can not, like the egg-cell, develop from itself numerous generations of cells, of which some transform themselves into skin-cells, some into flesh-cells, and others into bone-cells, etc. But instead, the nerve-cell, which is formed for the highest activities of life, possesses the capacity to feel, to will, to think. It is a true mind-cell, an elementary organ of mental activity. Correspondingly, it has an extremely complex minute structure. Innumerable filaments of exceeding fineness, which may be compared to the numerous electric wires of a great central telegraph station, traverse (crossing each other again and again), the finely granulated protoplasm of the nerve-cell, and pass into branched processes, which proceed from this mind-cell, and connect with other nerve-cells and nerve-fibres. It is scarcely possible to trace, even approximately, the tangled paths of these filaments in the fine substance of the protoplasmic body. We thus have before us a highly complex apparatus, the more minute structure of which we have hardly begun to know, even with the help of our strongest microscope, and the significance of which we rather guess than know. Its complex mechanism is capable of the most intricate physical functions. But even this elementary organ of mental activity, of which there are thousands in our brain, is only a single cell. Our whole intellectual life is but the sum of the results of all such nerve-cells, or mind-cells." *

* *Evolution of Man*, i. p. 129.

From this passage it will be seen that ascertained facts are given in harmony with previous descriptions; but that while naming some as sensory, others as motor, there is no distinct evidence for classifying certain cells as "mind-cells." Along with the admission of our comparative ignorance of the minute structure of the cell, is the assertion that this cell "possesses the capacity to feel, to will, to think." This latter statement is advanced without any trace of scientific evidence, and has no better substratum on which to rest than the admission that man not only feels, but also thinks and wills. Further, when we recall the singular variety of situation in which these cells are found, as they lie within the spinal canal, subordinate centres, and the brain, the insufficiency of the whole theory of "mind-cells" is apparent. Still more conspicuous does this become when we turn to Hæckel's illustrative diagram, and read underneath it this description,—"A large branched nerve-cell, or 'mind-cell' from the brain of an electric fish." The investigator who makes in the directest manner statements as to thinking and willing, which he has not verified and can not verify; and who with undisturbed composure of mind proceeds to illustrate and support his position by giving a drawing of the "mind-cell of an electric fish," does almost every thing that can be done to discredit his testimony on scientific subjects.

Having now set forth the grounds on which I think it clearly shown that physiological science has done no more than identify sensory and motor cells; and that the search for the true "mind-cell" has proved a failure; I pass from this division of the subject with the acknowledgment that the front and back portions of the brain still present area for fresh research, and to this must be added the striking fact that in all the brains subjected to electric excitation these two portions have uniformly remained silent. These considerations may possibly hereafter afford valuable suggestions towards guidance of the work yet to be done in the investigation of brain structure and functions.

In view of the limits of the present discussion, I shall at this point pass over at once and directly to the region concerned with *the government of human conduct*, with the view of illustrating in what respects human life differs from merely animal life. On this single test,

I must here be content to rest an argument for the insufficiency of physiology, and the necessity for observation of our own experience, if we are to have an intelligible account of the most familiar characteristics of human life. By way of securing a sharp contrast serviceable for illustrative and argumentative purposes, I take an extract from Mr. Darwin. His statement is this,—"There is no evidence that any animal performs an action for the exclusive good of another." * Alongside of this statement, for the purpose of comparison and contrast, let me place this. It is an essential law of human life, having daily application, that man shall so act as to make the good of his fellowman the express end of his action. This is a law of moral life which we do not dream of applying to any lower order of beings, but which we do regard as binding on all men equally. Explicit testimony to this law of human life may be drawn from the philosophy of Greece and of China in times so remote as to precede the Christian era, or from the teaching of our Saviour, or from the daily life of men in any land in this nineteenth century. The contrast is thus sharp

* *Origin of Species*, 6th ed. p. 208.

enough, and it presents the most perplexing difficulty for physiologists of the school of Hæckel; while it affords the strongest line of evidence for that philosophy which accounts for the higher characteristics of human life by reference to mind as distinct from brain, and immeasurably higher in function.

Whether Mr. Darwin's account of animal conduct will be uniformly accepted by naturalists, need not concern us, as the possibility of dissension would not seriously affect the argument, the main stress of which must fall on these two points, that the law of pure benevolence is a law of human life, and that the mere recognition of this law (I do not say *obedience to it*, which is a stage further in advance), can not be included within the functions of brain.*

From what has been written by some naturalists as to the "benevolence" of animals, it is probable that some may be prepared to take exception to the statement of Mr. Darwin. There is no need for here entering upon discussion which might thus be raised, and which would entail the task of criticising mul-

* Whether some of the animals may possess an inferior order of mind, is a question which need not be here discussed.

titudes of statements made in a singularly loose and unscientific manner. There is not any more careful observer than Mr. Darwin, the whole record of whose observations gives confidence in his testimony, and his patient reflection on the real significance of what he has seen. We may, however, leave this matter to naturalists, that they may decide whether this conclusion as to animals requires some modification. The purpose of the present argument is to show that an authoritative law of benevolence does apply to human life, in direct contrast with the ordinary law of animal life, giving special force to the struggle for existence as witnessed in the history of the lower orders of beings.

One possible entanglement for the present argument must, however, be carefully shunned. In the comparison between man and animal, we are apt to diverge into a discussion of what men and animals severally *do*. This is a question considerably different from that now under discussion, and yet it lies in such close proximity as to afford the greatest facilities for confusion of thought. We are not here comparing what animals do, with what men do; we are comparing the actions of animals with what we *know men ought to do.* It is this question of *ought* which appears as the outstanding and distinguishing feature in human life, on which we are now seeking to direct attention with all the concentration which physiologists secure when the microscope is directed on brain tissue. The true feature here is elevation and complexity of *intellectual* action, and the possibility of assigning this to brain action. The question is no doubt concerned with conduct both in the animal, and in man,—but what we wish to ascertain is, how far action or conduct in the two cases throws light on the exercise of intelligence possible to man and to animal. It is admitted that to act on a law of benevolence requires a higher exercise of intelligence, than to act under a law of desire or sensitive impulse; and we wish to reach definite conclusions on two points; *first*, and subordinately, whether animals ever act on the higher law; *second*, and chiefly, whether such action does not involve as its condition an intellectual exercise of a higher order than can be assigned to brain. The former of these questions, subordinate to the present inquiry, may be left to naturalists. The second concerns us directly here, in the more important discussion as to man.

With the view of completing the defence against disturbing entanglement, it may be well further to insert here the explicit statement that men do very commonly act in neglect of the law of benevolence, and even in violation of it. The fact is too well known in society to be overlooked. It may be enough, however, in the present connection, to admit that men do often act like the animals; or, to state the fact more precisely in form, the animal nature is often found governing men, so as to make their action resemble that of the lower animals in the struggle for existence.

These lines of severance will now make clear what is our main question,—Is man capable of recognizing a higher law of life? Does a law of benevolence apply to him as a rational creature, as it can not apply in the history of the animals around us? And if this question be answered in the affirmative, does such answer imply the exercise of a higher power than can be scientifically assigned to brain cells?

That man recognizes a law of benevolence as determining personal conduct will not be formally disputed by any one. Yet so very much bearing on the present argument is involved in the interpretation to be assigned to this admission, that it is desirable to present at least in outline, the evidence on which the statement rests. If we look at the facts in view of the ordinary actions of the lower animals, a series of contrasts is presented. The animals are seen to compete with each other for what is a common object of desire, such as a favorite article of food; and to fight with each other for possession; the consequence is that the strongest and most daring get what they seek, while the weaker and more timid must be content with what is of less value for gratification of their desire. These facts are so conspicuous and so constant in their influence on the whole race of animals that the theory of the origin of species by descent founds upon them. A complete contrast appears in what man recognizes as the rule of his conduct, when he admits the obligation to benevolence. There is a reflective exercise concerned with the right and wrong in human conduct which regards it as a wrong thing for a man to snatch from another the enjoyment within his reach, or subvert his opportunity for happiness in order to increase his own pleasure. On the other hand, there is an exercise of thought which contemplates effort for the good of others as right, even extending the application of this law of moral life so far as to require self-denial, and, in circumstances of special importance, self-sacrifice, for the good of others. These are facts so elementary, that the statement of them would be felt to be uncalled for, were we not seeking to distinguish the elements of our ordinary experience. In accordance with what has been said, we are agreed in regarding it as a wrong done to another if we deprive him of enjoyment simply for the sake of our own satisfaction. Such conduct is what we condemn as *selfishness* in the agent, and a *wrong* to the sufferer. When on the contrary we subordinate personal pleasure in order to secure the happiness of another, we commend the benevolent disposition in which the act originates, and we honor attention shown to the rights of a fellowman.

As the contrary lines of conduct are so often followed, and even vindicated as permissible in the competitions of life, we need to show with some care that the law of benevolence is uniformly regarded as a law of human conduct even when its requirements are unfulfilled. This becomes obvious if we look along another line of observation. If we pass from what a man does to his fellowmen to what he is seen to expect of them, we at once perceive that the authoritative feature alleged to belong to the principle of benevolence is admitted by him. He resents the selfishness from which he has suffered, complains of the unmanly act which found its pleasure in his injury, and an appeal to public opinion, on any occasion sufficiently important to involve a question of the interests of society, at once calls forth general condemnation of the selfish act as a real injustice.

That such a form and direction of thought belongs naturally to man has been further shown by the ready assent of the young to the law of benevolence, and their unhesitating test of their seniors by reference to it. If their irritability and resentment have been stirred, it may be difficult to gain their assent to the special application of the law of benevolence in the circumstances. This, however, is only an example in early life, of what we find in more advanced years, that it is hard to do the right, and easy to excuse the wrong we do, while resenting the wrong done to us. But, apart from exciting causes, and simply in the exercise of a quiet reflection, the child recognizes the duty of benevolence; and, notwithstanding the disadvantages of weakness and inexperience, proceeds to test others by this standard, and is felt by others to be powerful by reason of the force belonging to the law, however superior in years, and in authority may be the persons of whom the child expects that he be kindly treated. These are in very condensed form the facts of human life, which are as outstanding as the contrary facts insisted upon as characteristic of animal life. We need an explanation which shall put the nature of man as truly in contrast with the nature of the animal, while it is at the same time allowed that man has an animal nature which may operate to the influence of his conduct, in neglect of this higher law of intelligence.

Now the most advanced results of physiological science carry no explanation of this simple, ordinary fact, man's recognition of a law of benevolence as authoritative. After we have assigned full value to the *sensibilities* of a physical nature overspread with a sensitive nerve-system; after we have made account of the motor activity possible to an animal possessed of a complicated muscular system controlled by motor nerves, we have not come near a region in which the reflective process takes place which applies the law of benevolence for the regulation of conduct. We discover within the range of physiological possibility, sensitiveness to impression from without, and to the influence of the cravings and appetites of a nature requiring support and satisfaction, and impelling power which urges to action for the sake of present satisfaction. All these things we find easily explained under the teaching of physiology; but we have no explanation of the act of intelligence in perceiving a law of benevolence and owning submission to it. We do not even find a scientific account of the subordinate intellectual exercises involved in the application of the law of benevolence when recognized.

There is a form of discrimination here, including the distinction of men as persons, the claims involved in personal rights, and the phase of individual duty ascertained while contemplating the circumstances in the midst of which it is needful to act. All this is outside the range of the formulated results of physiological research. There can be no hesitation in accepting all that has been established as to nerve-sensibility,—the subjection of human life to the interaction of external influences,—and the inevitable forms of experience which result in individual history. But we see in these, only conditions in the midst of which man by exercise of his intelligence is to undertake the management of life on a higher level than that of animal life. We clearly recognize the laws of motor activity, including the full bearing of outward influences, and inward tendencies upon human action. But with these things we see what is meant when it is recognized that intellect must govern passion: while we see physiological science laying open to us only the laws of passion, and not the law for its government. We admit the convincing nature of the evidence by which it is shown that our nature with all the special phases of individuality, often involving strange perils and perplexities, has been inherited by us, gathering within the boundaries of our life a task which we would willingly have shunned. We perceive in this a science of the specialities of individual nature, standing alongside the science explaining the common characteristics of man which come within the range of physiological research. But it is beyond this, that the problem arises concerning the moral government of life, so that equally what is common, and what is peculiar to man shall be regulated according to rational law. For this all see to be true, excepting always cases of manifest infirmity and disorder, that equally the common and the special powers of the individual are to be regulated by the law of benevolence. There are no exemptions for special temperament, whatever diversities there may be in the task which application of the law may involve for some. The *ought* has ascendency over human life;* the bare perception of this grand reality, taken with all the distinctions involved in its application to personal conduct,

* See Appendix XIII.

and all the forms of personal control exercised for its fulfilment, lies apart from the discoveries of physiology. In these things we see most clearly what mind is, and what mind does in the management of human life. We discover clearly thus what it is which makes human life superior to the life of the animals around us; what it is which makes the best in human life stand essentially connected with the subordination of the animal nature to a higher nature within; and in what respect it stands true that physiology is a science of only a part of our nature, and that the lower, because the subject part. In this man knows, apart from all science, and quite independently of philosophy too, that he has a higher life, working, rejoicing, and advancing to nobler excellence, just as he governs his body, keeping it in subjection, while revering an ideal of moral and spiritual excellence towards the attainment of which it is the duty and honor of humanity to strive.

LECTURE VIII.

RELATION OF SCIENCE TO OUR CONCEPTIONS OF DIVINE INTERPOSITION FOR MORAL GOVERNMENT IN THE WORLD.

THE view given in previous lectures of the most prominent features of the recent advances in scientific knowledge most intimately concerning our religious conceptions of the origin and government of the world, may afford some aid towards forming a judgment of the points of contact and apparent conflict. A brief summary will afford the best introduction to the lines of inquiry with which the present discussion may be brought to a close.

First, as to the inorganic in the universe, recent investigations favor the conclusion that neither the matter in the world, nor the energy, can be increased or diminished by operation of any laws known to apply to such existence. The laws under which these two forms of being hold their place in the world involve only change of distribution and relation. Both matter and energy are, however, perpetually undergoing change or transformation, and whether the change be for the better or for the worse in the history of the universe as a whole, the fact of unceasing change in subordination to fixed law, is clear evidence that matter and energy are not eternal or self-subsisting, but are dependent on some transcendent existence imposing the laws determining their relations.

Second, as to organized existence, recent researches go to prove that there is in all animals a measure of adaptability to surrounding conditions of life, providing for "adaptive changes" in the organism, which become fixed, and are transmitted to succeeding generations of the same order under the law of heredity. On warrant of the evidence for this, it is to be taken as certain that the various orders of animals now familiar to us did not at first come into being with all the characteristics now pertaining to them. The law of their life has provided for a progression in development, in accordance with which we have distinct orders of the pigeon, the dog, and the horse, with variations in animals of every class. This law of development, applicable to all animal life, admits of greater or less diversity of result in the history of distinct races, according to the complexity of the organism.

Third, as to the relations of different orders in the scale of animal life, it is proved that all vital organism has been modelled on a common plan as appears in the arrangement and functions of the nerve system, providing for sensibility and motor activity. In accordance with this, we find in different orders of animal life not merely analogies or resemblances in structure, but homologies or examples of complete identity of structure and function. Thus the brain, and the two sets of nerve lines, namely sensory and motor, are the same in nature and functions in all animals, from the frog to man inclusive, and they differ only in complexity of arrangement within the central organ, and extent of ramification of the nerve lines. Diversity of nature thus far appears in the relative complexity of organism. This is a conclusion which assigns to man his place in the scale of animal life; that is, in so far as we regard man exclusively by reference to his animal nature, he stands highest in the scale of organism,—first in rank, judged simply by complexity of brain structure, and minuteness of nerve system.

Fourth, in respect of moral life, that is, ability to contemplate a law of life absolutely authoritative as well as universally applicable amongst intelligent beings,—such for example as the law of benevolence; ability to control the whole animal nature so as to subject it to this higher law of benevolence; ability to strive after the harmonizing of all dispositions and actions in accordance with the law of benevolence,—man occupies a distinct place in the order of beings existing in the world, no other living being standing associated with him. There are innumerable forms of organized being in the world; but only a single representative of moral life in it. No being save man contemplates a general law of life, making its fulfilment a deliberate end of action; no being save man possesses a conception of duty or oughtness, which, if it be regarded simply as an intellectual exercise, can be apprehended only under application of a law of conduct such as benevolence. That man stands entirely alone in these respects, and is, therefore, to be ranked as a distinct order of being, appears from the following definite lines of evidence: no animal contemplates a general law of conduct, or intelligible rule of life applicable for the government of the order to which it belongs; no animal subordinates physical impulse at the bidding of such a law; no animal aims at the perfecting of its nature under a general conception of the excellence of its own nature, as dog, horse, or ape. Therefore we conclude that man alone of all living beings known to us in this world is a moral being.

Taking now these four aspects of existence as known to us in this world,—without advancing to deal directly with the phases and conditions of religious life,—the whole four can be freely accepted by religious men in strict harmony with all the requirements of religious thought. The three first named are distinct advances in the history of physical science, and will be generally admitted to include the most important accessions to our knowledge of the physical universe having any bearing on the conceptions lying at the basis of religious thought. The fourth is the product of philosophical inquiry, proceeding in accordance with direct observation of personal experience, and by means of simple analysis of our intelligent activity as that is concerned with the government of personal life, especially in view of the relations subsisting in society. This last as a philosophic conclusion, not attained by physiological research, not properly any part of physical science, but reached only by distinguishing properly certain contents of our every-day thought, may be liable to rejection from those who rely only on the methods peculiar to physical science. But such treatment of the propositions has no bearing on their truth; as denial of them will not deliver any man from the obligations of benevolence, or exempt him from the demands of his fellowmen, requiring that in seeking his own satisfaction he shall not be selfish, and certainly not harsh, as if the strongest might have all they desire, and the weakest must be content to wait on their pleasure. Denial of the recognition of a law of benevolence will not exempt him from the experience consequent on the expectations of his fellowmen as they seek help for the suffering, or sympathy for the sorrowful, or rescue for the perishing. Though what has been said as to the law of benevolence implies that it is universally authoritative, there is no express philosophic theory here introduced as to the mode by which this knowledge is attained, or the grounds on which its universality is asserted. The bare fact that each man expects his fellowman to be benevolent is enough for the present purpose. The simple declaration that the man who seeks only his own gratification, setting at defiance all the rights of his fellowmen, is unworthy the name of man and acts a brute's part, is all that any one needs who would make good the argument that human nature is distinct from that of the brutes. No man can escape the obligation to benevolent disposition; no man except the man of gross character attempts to live as if he regarded the violation of it as capable of vindication. These two things being so, the testimony is as strong as that establishing the elementary truths of science, which demonstrates that man owns a universal moral law, and so distinguishes himself from the animals. The conditions of human life are too clearly recognized, and too constantly insisted upon in ordinary society, to allow cover for ambiguities, and denials which would favor the position of those who accept only what is ascertained by the methods of physiological investigation. Hence it happens that popular favor runs deeply and strongly for the kind and good; and science itself must yield when the testimony of the race is uniform.

Before closing this inquiry, it is desirable to pass over from the outstanding conceptions of science and philosophy, to distinctive and prominent conceptions belonging to religious thought, with the view of considering whether these can be held in harmony with the teaching of science. Of these, reference may be made specially to two which encounter opposition on professedly scientific grounds:—Miracle as an evidence of the Messiahship of our Lord Jesus Christ; and the efficacy of Prayer in the economy of spiritual life. These two conceptions have encountered strong opposition on the allegation of inconsistency with the unchangeableness of the laws of nature. It becomes, therefore, an important part of the present investigation, to ascertain how far these two articles of Christian faith, miraculous testimony to the divinity of our Saviour, and habitual answer to the prayer offered to God by those who approach Him in the merit of the Redeemer, are consistent with the teaching of science. These two conceptions are naturally included in the one question as to the compatibility with the laws of nature of the interposition of supernatural agency for attainment of moral and spiritual ends in the history of the world.

First in order stands the question of MIRACLE as involved in the evidence of divine power and authority given by our Lord, during His sojourn in this world to accomplish the great work of redemption.* The testimony of miracle as presented in the historical narrative of Christ's life is frequent and abundant in variety; and its connection with His work for the redemption of sinful men is everywhere proclaimed. It is impossible to contemplate the scriptural testimony to the glory of Christ's nature without including miracle as a conspicuous part of it; and it is equally impossible to detach this testimony

* The limits of the present discussion make it impossible to include a wider range; but this really embraces the whole question of the miracles of Scripture.

from relation to the mediatorial work of the Redeemer as concerned with the pardon of sin, and restoration of man to holiness of character. It thus becomes an essential test of the validity of Christian evidence to settle the compatibility of miracle with the knowledge now possessed of the laws of nature.

It is not necessary here to discuss the credibility of miracles, as affected by the question whether there can be sufficiency of testimony to support the occurrence of a miracle,—a question which has engaged an amount of attention disproportionate to its intellectual worth. The suggestion of the question was nothing better than an example of misleading ingenuity, allowed to stand on the page on which it was indited in manifest violation of the laws of evidence and the essential conditions of human knowledge. The value of testimony does not depend on the nature of the thing to which it applies, but on the character of the witness, and the opportunity for observing and testing the facts described. There are, for example, a series of surgical operations being performed in Edinburgh for removal of tumors (Ovariotomy), and being repeated at intervals of two or three weeks, which have hitherto been declared by the profession to be impossible without sacrifice of life; and yet they are successfully accomplished, leaving only an exceedingly small percentage of death. The whole combined testimony of preceding ages has been against the possibility of such operations; but this is a consideration of no value whatever in view of the testimony of the surgeons who take part in the hazardous and responsible, but most beneficent work, and of those professional men who have come from France, and Russia, and other lands, to witness the operation, and of citizens well acquainted with patients who have been delivered from a burdened life, overshadowed with prospect of early death. The laws of evidence are too well understood to call for abstract reasoning as to the credibility of the witnesses who are at present giving their testimony to the scientific world, of the successful repetition of an operation hitherto believed to be impossible. The bearing of such an illustration on the discussions raised concerning the credibility of the evidence of our Lord's disciples to the miracles He performed is obvious. Nor is there need for occupying time in trampling out the beaten straw by lingering over the argument that no evidence can be sufficient to establish a miracle, *because* a miracle is contrary to common experience; for, it is obvious that a miracle must be contrary to common experience, since that which is matter of common experience can not be a miracle, but must be an event determined by some law of nature. The uniformity of the laws of nature is even a necessary condition for the evidential value of miracles.

We pass to the real merits of the question in discussing the possibility of the miracles of Christ without violation of any of the laws of nature as ascertained by the most recent advances of science.

The miracles of Jesus Christ profess to be supernatural interpositions for accomplishment of an immediate benevolent purpose, while in combination they afford a body of evidence testifying to the power and benevolent mission of a divine Saviour of the sinful. Their directly benevolent aim is conspicuous throughout. Jesus never performs any wonderful work for display of power; when a desire is indicated for signs in the heavens, these are refused; when His own wants are concerned, there is no exercise of power to deliver Himself from suffering; but when a poor sufferer appeals for deliverance, He is ready to act; or when the feeble, oppressed condition of one who has been a long time in this case comes under His eye, He is moved to compassion and gives unexpected deliverance even without intervention of a request. All this is done, not as if it were any part of the divine purpose to keep men exempt from suffering, nor as if it were inconsistent with the divine benevolence to allow its return and continuance, for He is at pains to warn that even a worse thing may come; but as if deliverance from suffering were in harmony with His mission, and peculiarly appropriate as illustrative of a Saviour's design as well as of His divine power. By way of sign He would rescue from disease, in order thereby to point to a grander deliverance, even from sin which causes all the world's sorrow.

The question here calling for attention is, How do these miracles stand related to the laws of nature which we now recognize as fixed and unchangeable? The *first* portion of the answer must be that they are incapable of explanation under these laws. They are veritable examples,—referring for the present exclusively to their nature, not to the evidence on which we acknowledge that they occurred,—they are veritable examples of results incapable of being attained under the operation of natural law. The effects secured were indeed only such as would have been attained had medical science been able to accomplish the result, for the great majority of them belong to the region in which the grand healing art works out its beneficent contribution to human well being. But in respect of the mode of their execution they were in *no sense analogous* to what is achieved by unexpected advance in scientific knowledge and skill. There was nothing in the whole course of our Lord's life, bearing resemblance to the work of him who laboriously ponders the varied aspects of some selected form of disease, and ultimately attains to skill in a new mode of treatment, or a dangerous and difficult form of operation. The word spoken to the leper or the paralytic; the anointing of the eyes with clay and sending the blind man with his clay-covered eyelids to wash in a pool; the command to Jairus's daughter, "Maid, arise;" and the call to the man of

Bethany, "Lazarus, come forth,"—present no likeness to the conduct of one merely exercising a deeper knowledge of the remedial measures which are constantly being employed in some mode or other for relief of suffering. What we witness in the varied forms of His works is supernatural intervention, exercise of divine authority and power. There is no competent vindication of the sacred narrative by reduction of our Lord's works to the level of those forms of knowledge and skill which are within the reach of human discovery. The sacred writings offer no suggestion pointing in this direction; Christian faith, in the defence it offers for its recognition of the miraculous in Christ's life, does not shelter itself behind such a poor breastwork, as that which is gained by eliminating the supernatural,—seeking to defend itself by surrendering all that is distinctive of the God-man, who not only spake as man never spake, but who with profuse liberality performed works of healing which made the ears of the nation to tingle, compelling reluctant witnesses to testify, that it was never so seen in Israel. The supernatural works of Jesus belong to the same place in history, as that which records the supernatural attributes belonging to His personality.

To the question, How do the works of Jesus stand related to the laws of nature? the *next* portion of the answer is that they do not conflict with these laws in any intelligible sense. The believer in Christ's miracles, as he meets the manifest requirements of science, may fairly ask of scientific critics that they state any law of nature which was violated in any example of the Saviour's benevolent doings, in a sense of the word "violation" which conflicts with the indubitable teaching of science concerning the unchangeableness of the laws of nature. It might well suffice for exposition of Christian thought at an earlier period of Bible interpretation when the sole object was to set forth the transcendent grandeur of Christ's works, to represent a miracle as "a violation of the laws of nature," meaning thereby to concentrate on the fact that equally by its character, and by profession of the agent, it was a work which ordinary power was insufficient to explain. By parity of reasoning, it may equally be allowed that a legitimate course is followed, and an important service is rendered to the advance of Christian evidence, if it be urged by scientific men that a violation of the laws of nature is inconsistent with what is now ascertained as to the government of the physical world. This collision between old forms of statement and new forms of test is a gain to all interests concerned. It must press into notice the inquiry as to the sense in which the old terminology was employed, and also the sense in which this new test is presented. If this comparison be prosecuted to its final result, no Christian believer will find himself disturbed by apprehension of a possible call to conflict with science, and no scientific men will feel themselves drawn into antagonism with the accredited forms of Christian belief as to the miraculous. A few carefully stated propositions should help towards making this clear, if only these can be so drawn as to meet the demands of science, and also accurately represent Christ's life.

The testimony of science dealing with the evidence open to observation is that the laws of nature, such as the laws of gravitation, transmutation of energy, and the development and support of living organism, are fixed and unchangeable, so that persistent antagonism to them is only conflict of a weaker force with a stronger which must end in disaster or destruction to the weaker. Over against this we do not find it possible to place any statement, either in the form of direct affirmation, or of inference deducible from the implications of Christ's actions or words, which can be regarded as directly contradictory. On the contrary the deeds and sayings of Christ carry a multitude of suggestions in strict harmony with this general teaching of science. When He would indicate to His hearers how they are guided in their judgment by the uniformity of natural law, He points to the signs which they interpret in the aspect of the atmosphere morning and evening. When the suggestion is placed before Him that He should cast Himself from an eminence in token of His superiority to ordinary risks, He does not hint at a suspension of the law of gravitation, but teaches that man should not transgress the divine will by rashly exposing himself to danger. When He would teach men to combine labor and trust, He points them to the uniform provision for the clothing and adorning of the vegetable world which can not in any measure care for itself. And so we might proceed, were there any need for multiplying evidence as to a feature of Christ's teaching manifest to every Bible reader.

The record of Scripture presenting the narratives of Christ's miracles does not at any time represent our Saviour as interposing to stay for a brief period the action of fixed law, or to prevent the application of such law in the history of a particular individual. In all these wonders of healing nothing more happens as to actual *result*, having a general bearing on procedure in the physical world, than does happen when a cure of a critical phase of disease is accomplished by some newly discovered appliance at command of medical art. These two cases are essentially different as to *mode* of action, but they are strictly identical as to *result*, and this identity amounts to a demonstration of harmony with scientific requirements, as these actually guide men to the discovery of new methods. That there is identity of result only *in some cases* does not affect the argument, but arises from the essential features of the comparison, as a product of supernatural intervention must transcend what is ultimately attained by laborious processes of human research. But that there is in any case an identity of result under the very different conditions, is an indication that supernatural intervention is not an interference with the laws of nature such as would be involved in their suspension or subversion. There is a great difference between recovery from suspended animation and resurrection from the dead as in the case of Lazarus, but the fixed order of the universe is no more disturbed in the latter case than in the former.

A further consideration bearing on the miracles of Christ needs to be stated, though it comes more directly into relation with philosophy than with science properly so called. Every one of these miracles was performed avowedly for moral ends, and under application of moral conditions, while for immediate physical effects. There is moral law as well as physical law, and our Saviour subordinates the latter to the former in determining the use He makes of supernatural agency. The evidence of this is interwoven through the very texture of the narrative, so that an attempt to sever His miracles from their moral purpose can result only in tearing the narrative into fragments,—mutilating the record which must be studied and interpreted as it has been put into our hands. Moral law is as unchangeable as physical law, though the character and form of its sway differ from those of physical law, and it is easier for man wilfully to violate the higher law of life than to violate the lower. Yet so closely are the higher and lower connected in human history, that the easy violation of moral law is followed by painful consequences under the reign of physical law. It lay within the purpose of Jesus to deliver from both, and it is only in recognition of this combined or complex purpose that we discover the rational basis on which supernatural deliverance from disease becomes a natural vehicle for presenting to rational beings requisite evidence of divine intervention on their behalf as they are entangled in the disastrous consequences of violating unchangeable moral law. If on other grounds it be apparent that supernatural interference for restoration of health or life does not involve interference with physical law by which the government of the universe could be in any degree affected; on the grounds now contemplated we come to recognize a harmony of higher and lower orders of fixed law bearing on the history of the human race, and for this harmony of law our Saviour manifested a supreme concern.

With these brief statements before us, we are now prepared for turning in a different direction to ascertain what is the special view of miracle which has found currency within some scientific circles, carrying the explanation of intense antipathy to its acknowledgment, and unhesitating declaration that the whole body of scientific teaching, and even the characteristics of scientific method, are adverse to the very conception of miracle. For the purpose now in view it may be well to present in close connection the successive utterances of a single author, who may be taken as representative of a class. The work of Professor Schmidt on *The Doctrine of Descent and Darwinism* will supply illustrations of the kind to which reference has been made, as this author states at the outset that the doctrine of descent finds its antagonists among those "who perceive, more or less distinctly, the danger with which the new doctrine threatens their standpoint of miracle." * From this allusion it appears that he regards a doctrine of descent as opposed to what he describes as an "incomprehensible act of creation." † Accordingly he celebrates the praises of this theory in these terms,—"it interprets by a single principle those great phenomena which without its aid remain a mass of unintelligible miracles." ‡ In harmony with these utterances he speaks of gradual evolution of the organs of special sense, such as the organs of hearing and smell, as giving a negative to "the sudden and incomprehensible origination of these organs in an immediate state of completion." §

These few extracts may suffice to indicate the mental attitude of those who show aversion to the acknowledgment of miracle. With Schmidt the "miraculous" is another name for the incomprehensible; to him the suggestion of miracle is disagreeable as implying the impossibility of scientific explanation. If these things be kept in mind, it will be clear how widely apart this notion is from the Christian conception of miracle. The one

* p. 6. † p. 11. ‡ p. 12. § p. 151.

view is that observational science can make no account of miracle: the other is that thought concerning a supernatural Being really involves the conception of miracle. Science can assign no place to the incomprehensible, can make no account of it. Religion finds a higher sphere of comprehensibility in the action of supernatural power. The two positions are radically distinct, and do not come into actual conflict. Hence religion has no opposition to the view of miracle just stated, which amounts to little more than a negative definition of science. To say that science can take no account of the miraculous, is only in other words to say that science is explanation of natural phenomena by recognition of the action of natural causes, consequently the miraculous does not come within the boundaries of science. This is self-evident, and on this footing theology has no account to make of what is only a semblance of opposition, involving no real conflict. Creation, for example, can not come within the compass of observational science; but creation may nevertheless be a rational conception in dealing with a purely rational problem, which does not at all belong to physical science. In the same manner it appears that the whole series of our Lord's miracles are outside the area of science, which, as it has nothing of authority to advance against them, has not even a basis on which to offer any testimony concerning their possibility.

One topic more requires to be briefly considered as constituting an essential of religious thought, namely the acknowledgment of divine interposition for the answer of PRAYER. Our question is, How this conception of divine answer to prayer stands related to scientific thought concerning the government of the world by fixed law? If the laws of nature are fixed, how can the government of the world allow for fulfilment of human desire as expressed in supplication? The question to be discussed has two sides, the one concerned with the conditions on which an answer to prayer is expected; the other with the exact significance of the scientific conception of the government of the world by fixed law. If there be a rational basis for prayer as encouraged by the teaching of Scripture, there can be no such dilemma as would be implied in supposing that law is fixed yet not fixed, or that law is unchangeable in all cases save in the history of the man of prayer, in whose behalf the laws of nature are liable to be held in check. There may be among Christian men considerable diversity in the clearness of apprehension with which they grasp the meaning of the divine promise to answer prayer; but there is no one taught by the Scriptures as to the privilege of prayer, who thinks of it as implying that the laws of the universe are liable to be held in suspension because the desires of his heart are rising to God in humble, earnest supplication. The man trained to recognize this truth affecting God's government that "He maketh His sun to rise on the evil and on the good; and sendeth rain on the just, and on the unjust," does not readily fall into the mistake of supposing that all the laws of the universe are at His bidding, because of the divine encouragement to prayer. The Christian prays only under divine warrant, and this does not convey any such suggestion.

First, then, we can clear away at once the cruder thoughts of the unintelligent believer in the power of prayer; and those of the scientific objector to prayer, who is not instructed in scriptural doctrine. Prayer does not imply a probable reversal of the laws of nature; but it does imply a moral government in the midst of the physical world, and the subordination of the physical to the moral under regulation of an all-wise and almighty Ruler. The question before us concerns this subordination, and the possibilities which it implies.

Towards the attainment of exact conceptions here the first requisite is a clear understanding of the scientific doctrine of the government of the world by fixed law. In whatever sense we take the word "*law*" as applicable to God's government of the universe, there is no law which is fluctuating, or liable to have one signification at one time, and a quite different signification at another time; a narrower range of application at one period, and a wider range at a later. Such fluctuation would imply a suspension of a law of nature, and the conception of such a thing is inconsistent with absolute rational government, alien equally to the principles of science and of religion. Laws physical, moral, and spiritual are equally fixed laws.

But the laws of the universe are a harmony, and in the midst of the interdependence of laws distinct in character, the harmony of the whole is secured by the subordination of physical law to moral and spiritual. It is in the midst of this harmonized relationship of the diverse laws of the divine government that the spirit of prayer lives, and makes good its rational consistency. And it is only on condition of acknowledgment of diverse laws, including moral with physical, that the scientific man can interpose any criticism as to the efficacy of prayer. Any denial of a moral government in the midst of the physical universe, under sway of a God of righteousness, places an objector entirely out of the sphere in which criticism can proceed. Physical law determining conditions of bodily life is fixed law; moral law deciding the conditions of right conduct in intelligent life is fixed law; spiritual law deciding the conditions of fellowship with the Father of our spirits is fixed law. The believer in the Bible has no hesitancy in acknowledgment of all this; he is a believer in fixed law in a higher and grander sense than scientific teaching indicates, and he believes in the harmony of all existence under an unchangeable government, notwithstanding all the wrong doing in the world, and the dreadful misery resulting from it. His belief in the harmony of the universe rests on his belief in the fixedness of law physical as well as moral, and moral as well as physical.

But the *fixedness* belonging to various orders of law, subsisting in a state of interdependence, and involving subordination of lower to higher, needs some more exact interpretation. The fixedness of law, physical, intellectual, moral, and spiritual, in no case involves fixedness of result, but *varying results according to diversity of conditions.* There is fixedness of physical law, but withal there is diversity of weather, and seasons, and harvests, and that because a variety of conditions are harmonized under fixed law. There is fixedness of intellectual law in accordance with which accuracy of thought is determined, but diversity of result according to the materials with which we deal. And so it is with moral and spiritual law, providing for the regulation of our higher life.

What then needs to be pondered by way of reaching an ampler interpretation of the formula of "fixed law" is that it does not in any case imply an iron rigidity of result, an undeviating uniformity of occurrence. There is no region in which perpetual change can be more accurately postulated than in the physical world. But there is order and system in these changes, admirably illustrated in the weather forecasts of the present advanced stage of physical science, which are attainable only by continual watching of shifting conditions with application of fixed law to the appearance of wind and cloud and rain. But there are no forecasts without these two things, fixed laws and varying conditions for their application. With the wider generalization which admits of recognition of fixed law, there is always the narrower, concerned with variable conditions to which the wider is to be applied. So it is under moral law, and so under spiritual. So also does it hold when our observation is directed on interdependence of two orders of law, such as the moral and physical. This combination we have in human life, as it is subjected to both. Physical law reigns in human history as illustrated by the laws of health, which are fixed irrespective of moral law, so that sewerage gas will be prejudicial to health, apart from the moral character of a man. Moral law reigns in human life, and truthfulness in utterance, or justice in action, will maintain a harmony of the inner life, whether outwardly there be poverty or wealth. These two orders of law are independent, yet interwoven in their application to the complex life of man. Immorality will find its accompaniment in physical disorder; the repentance which has healing power within the mind will not heal the body, yet may there be advance in moral life by reason of the weakness and suffering which repentance can not remove. Such is at once the independence and the interdependence of physical and moral law, in accordance with the fixedness of law in each case, and the harmony of both under one government, by means of subordination of the physical to the moral.

There are thus *two spheres*, physical and moral, but *one life*, brought to harmony under the laws of both spheres. What then is the bearing of this distinction of spheres on the problem of the efficacy of prayer, viewing the question only in the light of science and philosophy? An obvious bearing, in so far as the conditions of physical and moral life are set forth and distinguished; but no determining value for interpretation of the possible influence of prayer as concerning a life subject at once to physical and moral conditions. Prayer can be exercised in accordance with scientific teaching, only by intelligent recognition of the physical conditions of life; in accordance with philosophy, only by intelligent acknowledgment of the subordination of physical life to moral. If then, we turn to the teaching of science, making account of all that it includes as to fixed laws applicable to ever-varying conditions, there is nothing in it to warrant the conclusion that there can be no interposition from a higher sphere in order to secure application of physical law for attainment of moral ends. The whole product of scientific investigation leaves clear the possibility of the administration of a moral government in accordance with subordination of physical law to the attainment of its higher ends. It does not help the understanding of the government of the world, but rather hampers our reflection, if it be suggested that there are two spheres, physical and moral, and that the application of prayer is restricted to one of these spheres. Human life can not be so severed into parts; it is a unity self-regulated by harmony of submission to moral and physical law, and it must be governed by the Supreme Ruler in the harmonious application of these laws. There is no sphere of life into which the moral does not enter, and accordingly no sphere within which prayer, which necessarily rests on moral conditions, may not apply.

If next we pass to Scripture teaching concerning prayer, where alone we find full instruction on the subject, in precept, example, and a variety of encouragements, it will appear that the warrant for prayer is found exclusively in the divine promise, and that the application of that promise is to every phase of life, subject to moral conditions which are explicitly revealed. Prayer is a privilege divinely bestowed through the Saviour, in accordance with which fellowship with God is granted on the merits of the Redeemer. Its nature reveals the true harmony between God and the moral creature, as a reality transcending all physical existence and all knowledge coming from study of physical law. The accepting of this privilege, and the continuance of its exercise are the tokens of returning harmony of sinful man with the holy God. Elevation in the exercise by steadily extending inclusion of a wider circle of personal desire and activity within the area of conscious fellowship with God, is the advance of the moral nature into fuller harmony with God, and with the whole government of the universe. The teaching of Scripture which assures of all this, and guides man towards realization of it, clearly distinguishes between material and moral good, yet does not exclude the one any more than the other, but subordinates the physical to the moral, harmonizing the two in recognition of the supreme importance of all that is moral. It does not exclude desire of temporal good, but restricts its illustration to desire of "daily bread,"—assures us that our Father knoweth we have need of such good, and will supply it,—and promises that having given most freely what is best, he will assuredly give that which is least.

If then it be said that the answer to prayer is a miracle of divine interposition in human history, of which science finds no trace, we do not marvel, for science does not extend its observations to the inclusion of what pertains to the higher life of man. If any man asks for evidence in an exclusively physical sphere that

God answers prayer, he asks that evidence should be discovered apart from the conditions involved. A more unscientific demand there could not be. When he refuses to admit that there can be any trustworthy evidence of the answer of prayer apart from the test he proposes, he either misunderstands the Christian doctrine of prayer, or he is criticising a conception of prayer other than the Christian one. If we turn to the philosophy of human life as subjected to moral law, and called to its perfect fulfilment, we do not find any thing but harmonious truth in the suggestion that God cares more for the moral life of man than for the physical universe. If we turn to Scripture, receiving its teaching as to prayer, we find that the promised interposition in man's behalf is even less an illustration of divine power than of Divine righteousness; an evidence that the Divine Ruler seeks righteousness above all things, for the entire significance of the exercise is this, trust in the holy One, and fellowship with Him through life. On this ground alone does He promise an answer to prayer, in this promise making moral conditions the essential test for use of the privilege, requiring the suppliant to subordinate to these all desire of material good. It is towards success in attaining true fellowship with Himself that God is ever giving promise of blessing. It is in full view of the transcendent value of a life of holiness, that the Supreme Ruler is daily condescending to stoop towards His children, that they may be helped in all that pertains to holiness of character and life. The Bible makes it essential to the government of the world, in harmony with fixed law, that God should be the hearer and answerer of the prayer of His intelligent creatures, always pointing to reliance on the Saviour's work as the test of the reality of the exercise, in the case of all who possess the written revelation of His will, in the glorious Gospel of Jesus Christ.

APPENDIX.

APPENDIX.

I.

Relations of Science and Religion. *Page* 34.

"He who contemplates the universe from the religious point of view, must learn to see that this which we call science, is one constituent of the great whole; and as such ought to be regarded with a sentiment like that which the remainder excites. While he who contemplates the universe from the scientific point of view, must learn to see that this which we call Religion is similarly a constituent of the great whole; and being such, must be treated as a subject of science with no more prejudice than any other reality. It behooves each party to strive to understand the other, with the conviction that the other has something worthy to be understood; and with the conviction that when mutually recognized this something will be the basis of a complete reconciliation."—Herbert Spencer, *First Principles*, p. 21.

II.

Spontaneous Generation. *Page* 54.

Professor Tyndall, describing his own experiments, says, "The experiments have already extended to 105 instances, not one of which shows the least countenance to the doctrine of spontaneous generation." Communicated to Royal Society of London, December 21, 1876.—*Nature*, vol. xv. p. 303.

III.

Energy and Force. *Page* 96.

The term Force is by many authors used as equivalent to Energy, rather than as a distinct term for the amount of Energy. Force is thus used by Sir W. R. Groves. "The term Force, although used in very different senses by different authors, in its limited sense may be defined as that which produces or resists motion." . . . "I use the term Force . . . as meaning that active principle inseparable from matter which is supposed to induce its various changes." . . . "All we know or see is the effect; we do not see Force—we see motion or moving matter."—*The Correlation of Physical Forces*, sixth edition, by the Hon. Sir W. R. Grove, pp. 10, 11.

IV.

All Organized Existence is Constructed on a Common Plan. *Page* 131.

"Biologists turn to the physical organization of man. They examine his whole structure, his bony frame, and all that clothes it. They resolve him into the finest particles into which the microscope will enable them to break him up. They consider the performance of his various functions and activities, and they look at the manner in which he occurs on the surface of the world. Then they turn to other animals, and taking the first handy domestic animal—say a dog,—they profess to be able to demonstrate that the analysis of the dog leads them, in gross, to precisely the same results as the analysis of the man; that they find almost identically the same bones, having the same relations; that they can name the muscles of the dog by the names of the muscles of the man, and the nerves of the dog by those of the nerves of the man, and that such structures and organs of sense as we find in the man, such also we find in the dog; they analyze the brain and spinal cord, and they find that the nomenclature which fits the one answers for the other. Moreover, they trace back the dog's and the man's development, and they find that at a certain stage of their existence, the two creatures are not distinguishable the one from the other; they find that the dog and his kind have a certain distribution over the surface of the world comparable in its way to the distribution of the human species. . . . . Thus biologists have arrived at the conclusion that a fundamental uniformity of structure pervades the animal and vegetable worlds, and that plants and animals differ from one another simply as modifications of the same great plan. Again they tell us the same story in regard to the study of function. They admit the large and important interval which, at the present time, separates the manifestations of the mental faculties observable in the higher forms of mankind, and even in the lowest forms, such as we know them, mentally from those exhibited by other animals; but, at the same time, they tell us that the foundations or rudiments of almost all the faculties of man are to be met with in the lower animals; that there is a unity of mental faculty, as well as of bodily structure, and that here also, the difference is a difference of degree and not of kind."—Lecture on "The Study of Biology," by Professor Huxley, *Nature*, vol. xv. p. 219. Delivered at South Kensington Museum, London, December 16, 1876. On the grounds here admirably summarized, it is clear that the whole organism of our world has been constructed on a common plan. This being true, similarities will appear in process of development, and in the structure and functions of different orders. This similarity, however, does not help us to explain "the large and important interval" which appears when mental characteristics are considered. It makes the diversity of mental power more difficult to explain by reference to organism, in fact contributing to the strength of evidence for mind as a form of existence distinct from organism.

V.

EMBRYOLOGY. *Page* 131.

I have not felt warranted to include in the text any summary of results secured by the important, but very difficult, investigations concerning the growth of animal life in the womb. This whole department of inquiry is in such an unfinished and uncertain state, that there is not warrant to found upon the evidence already obtained any general argument as to its bearing on a theory of evolution. The most competent observers admit that they are perplexed by facts ascertained, and confess that they can not as yet offer an explanation. To others all is as plain as possible; embryology supplies a convincing proof of the accuracy of an evolution theory; but these are scientific theorists who see by imagination, and are impatient of uncertainty. There are certain general considerations which must interpose difficulties in the way of constructing an argument from Embryology to evolution of species. (1) The action of environment before birth is altogether different from the action of environment after birth. (2) The theory of the evolution of species emphasizes this difference by insisting on the struggle for existence. (3) This difference being admitted, an argument from the one to the other can not hold. In the line of discovery the point of chief interest has been the fact that in some cases embryonic life shows a transition through lower forms analogous to lower orders of animal existence prior to reaching the mature stage when birth occurs. But in connection with the facts ascertained, two things are to be remarked. (1) Evidence of transition is most striking in the history of animal life developed external to the parental life, as in the transition from *larvæ* to *pupæ* among insects, and in the changes in the life of the tadpole. (2) If it be admitted that there is a common plan of structure for all organism, it is implied that there must be similarities in process of development. The question requiring answer, therefore, is whether in the gradual development from the germ, any further resemblance to lower orders appears than is to be anticipated on the admission of a common plan for organic structure. There are singular examples of transition. But there are no illustrations of uniform progress in the case of the higher orders such as would warrant the supposition that a history of evolution of the species can be read in the development of the fœtus. The supposition has, however, found currency in not a little of our scientific teaching. The incompleteness of this evidence may appear from examples. Take the tadpole. Huxley states the facts thus,—"The tadpole is first a fish, then a tailed amphibian, provided with gills and lungs, before it became a frog." This is development outside parental life, and does not belong to evidence in Embryology. Confining attention to embryonic life, let us take Huxley's statement, biologists "trace back the dog's and the man's development, and they find that at a certain stage of their existence, the two creatures are not distinguishable the one from the other." What is the inference to be drawn? If the two are not distinguishable, our powers of distinguishing are insufficient, for no biologist suggests that the two are alike. The difficulty of distinguishing two germs, or two examples of fœtus, is analogous to the difficulty which Darwin has pointed out of distinguishing the orders of dogs when they are six-days-old puppies, or the breed of three-days-old colt, or of nestling pigeons. At these stages, the animals may be so similar, that it is hardly possible to distinguish them, and yet in the full grown state they are quite different (Darwin's *Origin of Species*, sixth edition, p. 391). Mr. Darwin has presented the outstanding facts thus;—"The very general, though not universal, difference in structure between the embryo and the adult;—the various parts in the same individual embryo, which ultimately become very unlike and serve for diverse purposes, being at an early period of growth alike;—the common, but not invariable resemblance between the embryos or larvæ of the most distinct species in the same class;—the embryo often retaining whilst within the egg or womb, structures which are of no service to it, either at that or at a later period of life."

VI.

Non-advancement of Lower Orders. *Page* 158.

Mr. Darwin's answer to the difficulty put by Agassiz is this;—"On our theory the continued existence of lowly organisms offers no difficulty; for natural selection, or the survival of the fittest, does not necessarily include progressive development,—it only takes advantage of such variations as arise and are beneficial to each creature under its complex relations of life."—*Origin of Species*, sixth edition, p. 98. This wears the aspect of a limitation of the theory, and to that extent an acknowledgment of the force of the reasoning of Agassiz.

VII.

Protoplasm. *Page* 131.

"Protoplasm, simple or nucleated, is the formal basis of all life;" thus "all living forms are fundamentally of one character." "All the forms of Protoplasm which have yet been examined contain the four elements, carbon, hydrogen, oxygen, and nitrogen, in very complex union." Thus there is "a general uniformity in the character of the Protoplasm, or physical basis of life, in whatever group of living beings it may be studied."—Huxley's *Lay Sermons*, p. 142.

VIII.

Number of Species of Insects. *Page* 193.

Professor Huxley mentions that "Gerstæcker in the new edition of Broun's 'Thier-Reich' gives 200,000 as the total number of species of *Arthropoda*." In this connection Mr. McLauchlan, when claiming that there are 200,000 species of Insects, adds, "In one order alone (*Coleoptera*) it is estimated that 80,000 species have been described."—*Nature*, xv. p. 275.

IX.

Fertilization of Flowers by Insects. *Page* 170.

Dr. Hermann Müller's Observations are described in *Nature*, vol. xiv. p. 175; vol. xv. pp. 317, 473; vol. xvi. pp. 265, 507.

X.

Ants. *Page* 192.

Mr. McCook's Observations are summarized in *Nature*, vol. xvii. p. 433.

XI.

Likeness of the Ape's Brain to the Human Brain.
Page 225.

The close resemblance of the brain of the ape to that of man, has been held to prove that the ape comes next to man in intelligence. But the facts bearing on this suggestion are fitted to occasion serious perplexity to its upholders. First stands the resemblance of bodily structure as largely explaining similarity of brain. The results of electric stimulation of the monkey's brain lend additional force to this consideration. Again, facts are wanting to support the claim for superior intelligence in behalf of the monkey and ape. The habits of the ape in its natural state afford little evidence of an encouraging kind. The ape gathers together a few sticks for a nest, in comparison with which the work of very small birds presents marvels of architecture. And nest-building seems the highest evidence gathered from the natural habits of the animal, when we compare it with leaning the back against a tree for rest, or staunching the blood of a wound. In the captive state the ape gives no such evidence of superior intelligence as the similarity of its brain to the human, would lead us to expect, if brain structure afford the test of intellectual power. Even after allowance has been made for sudden transition from the wild state to the captive, the evidence of capability does not appear which the theory requires. The highest results reached by training monkeys, do not support a claim for intellectual superiority. These are mainly forms of mimicry, generally inferior to the efforts of some other animals.

Add to these considerations the evidence as to the singular intelligence shown by ants, and the theory which measures intellect by brain structure is placed at a great disadvantage. Whether science may not ere long point to some theory of mind connected with animal existence must be matter of uncertainty. If, however, the easy and familiar operations of our own intelligence are analyzed and classified; and if a statement of the ascertained functions of the brain is laid alongside, it will appear that nothing known to us in the action of brain, can supply a science of the operations of the human mind.

XII.

THE LARGE SIZED OR MULTIPOLAR CELLS. *Page* 257.

On the functions of the large sized cells, it seems desirable to add a few words as to the direction in which evidence as to their functions actually points. For this purpose, a further quotation is desirable, referring to the number of fibres or processes passing off from these large cells, distinguishing those which branch out into a fine net-work, and those which pass directly to a nerve fibre. "One at least of the processes of a multipolar nerve cell does not branch, but becomes directly continuous with a nerve fibre, and has been named the axial-cylinder process."—Professor Turner's *Human Anatomy,* i. 201. This taken with the facts given in Lecture VII, seems to favor the conclusions, (1) that the large cell spreads nerve energy through the tissue of the brain, while each has at least one direct line of communication with the system of nerve fibres; (2) that the large cell has intimate and extended relations with the motor system.

XIII.

The Conception of Duty. *Page* 273.

"Duty! Thou great, thou exalted name! Wondrous thought that workest neither by fond insinuation, flattery, nor by any threat, but by merely holding up thy naked law in the soul, and so extorting for thyself always reverence, if not always obedience,—before whom all appetites are dumb, however secretly they rebel,—whence thy original?"—Kant's *Critique of Practical Reason.*

For EU product safety concerns, contact us at Calle de José Abascal, 56–1°, 28003 Madrid, Spain or eugpsr@cambridge.org.

www.ingramcontent.com/pod-product-compliance
Ingram Content Group UK Ltd.
Pitfield, Milton Keynes, MK11 3LW, UK
UKHW010351140625
459647UK00010B/988

* 9 7 8 1 1 0 8 0 0 0 1 5 4 *